Cuaderno de actividades

⋆ Compañeros ⋆

Spanish for Communication
BOOK 1

Ruth A. Moltz, M.A.
Chair, Foreign Language Department
Southfield High School
Southfield, Michigan

Thomas A. Claerr, Ph.D.
Professor of Spanish
Henry Ford Community College
Dearborn, Michigan

AMSCO SCHOOL PUBLICATIONS, INC.
315 Hudson Street/New York, N.Y. 10013

When ordering this workbook, please specify either:
R 634 W *or* **Cuaderno de actividades, Compañeros, Spanish for Communication, Book 1**

ISBN 1-56765-453-3
NYC Item #56765–453–2

Printed in the United States of America

3 4 5 6 7 8 9 10   03 02

Preface

This **Cuaderno de actividades, Book 1,** is intended for independent student use as homework or as supplemental in-class practice. The exercises in the **Cuaderno** were specifically designed to provide focused practice of each grammar point presented in the **Compañeros, Spanish for Communication, Book 1** text.

Each vocabulary section and grammar point in the textbook has one or more corresponding exercises in the same sequence in the **Cuaderno.** At the end of some lessons is an optional section called **Diversión,** which allows the student to have fun while working with some aspect of the lesson.

Unidades II, III, and **IV** contain a **Leemos y contamos** section, which introduces a reading based on the vocabulary and grammar of the lesson and then gives students an opportunity to write something similar.

Following **Unidades II, III,** and **IV** is an important and useful review section called "Structure Review," which combines all the grammar and much of the vocabulary from the respective unit into integrated activities united by the theme of the core character Paulina and her friends.

Table of Contents

Nombre _____

⇒ Unidad I Lección 1 ⇐

Los saludos
Greetings

CONVERSACIÓN *Saying hello, Saying good-bye, Talking about health*

A. Say "hello" to the following people.

the little boy next door ____*Hola.*____

your teacher ____*Buenos días.*____

1. your friend _____

2. the person sitting next to you _____

3. your cousin or other relative _____

4. your pet _____

5. your boss _____

6. an adult visitor to class _____

7. the principal of your school _____

8. a new student _____

B. How do you greet someone formally at these times of the day?

10:00 P.M ____*Buenas noches.*____

1. 1:00 P.M. _____

2. 6:00 A.M. _____

3. 9:00 A.M. _____

4. 3:00 P.M. _____

5. 9:00 P.M. _____

6. 11:30 A.M. _____

7. 11:30 P.M. _____

8. 6:00 P.M. _____

C. Write a dialogue as it would occur between the following people.
- (Greet each other.)
- (Inquire about health of one person.)
- (Inquire about health of the other person.)
- (Say good-bye.)

1. a boy and a girl at a party

BOY _____

GIRL _____

BOY _____

GIRL _____

BOY _____

GIRL _____

BOY _____

GIRL _____

2. a man and a woman at the supermarket

MAN _____

WOMAN _____

MAN _____

WOMAN _____

MAN _____

WOMAN _____

MAN _____

WOMAN _____

3. a boy and a neighbor who asks about a friend who is ill.

BOY _____

NEIGHBOR _____

BOY _____

NEIGHBOR _____

BOY _____

NEIGHBOR _____

BOY _____

NEIGHBOR _____

CONVERSACIÓN *Saying please and thank you, Being courteous, Indicating knowledge and understanding, Asking for speech change, Asking for the word in Spanish/English*

D. Albert is going to spend his vacation with a Spanish-speaking family. Tell him what to say in the following situations.

1. He wants to ask someone who he or she is.

   _____

2. He steps on someone's toe.

   _____

3. He wants someone to repeat what he or she has said.

   _____

4. Someone has just said thank you to him.

   _____

5. He sympathizes with someone.

   _____

6. He doesn't know the answer to a question.

   _____

7. He wants to identify himself.

   _____

8. He doesn't understand what someone said.

   _____

9. He wants someone to talk louder.

   _____

10. He wants someone to speak slower.

    _____

11. Someone gives him something.

    _____

12. He wants to know how to say something in Spanish.

    _____

13. He wants to politely ask for something.

    _____

14. He wants to pass in front of someone.

    _____

15. He wants to know how to say something in English.

    _____

16. He wants to know what something means.

    _____

DIVERSIÓN

What are these people saying to each other?

1.

2.

3.

⋙ Unidad I   Lección 2 ⋘

Los nombres, las personas y las letras
Names, people, and letters

A. *Spanish names*   Many Spanish names are similar to English names. Others are the equivalent but are slightly different. Still others don't have an English equivalent. How many of these can you identify in English?

LAS MUCHACHAS

Alicia _____	Cristina _____
Alma _____	Diana _____
Ana _____	Dolores _____
Anita _____	Dorotea _____
Bárbara _____	Elena _____
Beatriz _____	Emilia _____
Blanca _____	Estela _____
Carlota _____	Eva _____
Carmen _____	Francisca _____
Carolina _____	Gloria _____
Catalina _____	Inés _____
Cecilia _____	Isabel _____
Clara _____	Josefina _____

Juana	_____	Mercedes	_____
Juanita	_____	Patricia	_____
Julia	_____	Paz	_____
Linda	_____	Pilar	_____
Lucía	_____	Raquel	_____
Luisa	_____	Rosa	_____
Luz	_____	Susana	_____
Manuela	_____	Teresa	_____
Margarita	_____	Verónica	_____
María	_____	Virginia	_____
Mariana	_____	Yolanda	_____
Marta	_____		

LOS MUCHACHOS

Alberto	_____	Domingo	_____
Alejandro	_____	Eduardo	_____
Alfonso	_____	Enrique	_____
Alonso	_____	Ernesto	_____
Álvaro	_____	Esteban	_____
Andrés	_____	Federico	_____
Antonio	_____	Felipe	_____
Arturo	_____	Fernando	_____
Benjamín	_____	Francisco	_____
Carlos	_____	Gregorio	_____
Daniel	_____	Guillermo	_____
Diego	_____	Jaime	_____

Javier _____	Pedro _____
Jesús _____	Ramón _____
Jorge _____	Raúl _____
José _____	Ricardo _____
Juan _____	Roberto _____
Luis _____	Salvador _____
Manuel _____	Santiago _____
Marcos _____	Teodoro _____
Mauricio _____	Timoteo _____
Miguel_____	Tomás _____
Nicolás_____	Vicente _____
Pablo _____	Víctor _____

VOCABULARIO   Las personas *People*

B. **¿Quién es?**   Describe each picture in Spanish in a complete sentence, using a form of **ser** and the definite article **el, la, los, las.**

Son las muchachas. _____

1. _____

2. _____

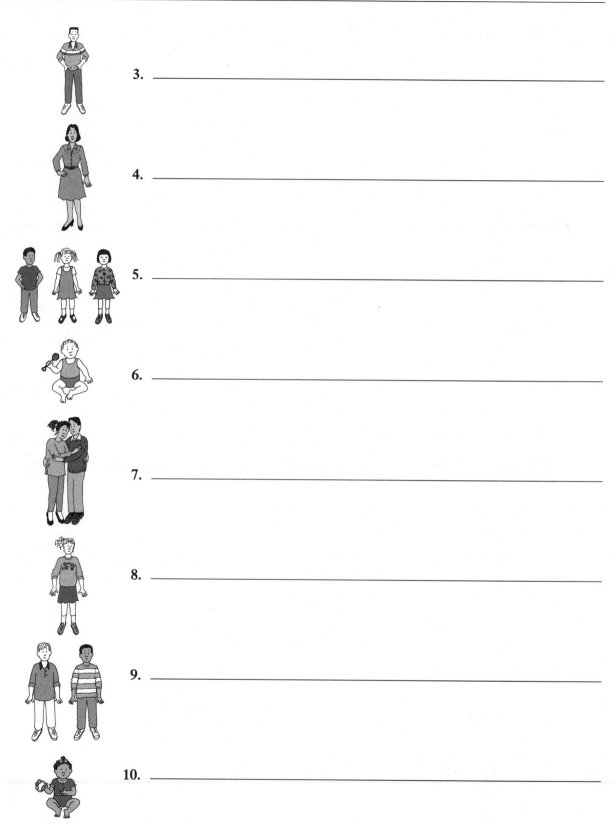

3. _____

4. _____

5. _____

6. _____

7. _____

8. _____

9. _____

10. _____

C. Answer each question with a complete sentence, using a form of **ser** and the indefinite article **un, una, unos, unas.**

¿Es un hombre?   ¿Son unos muchachos?

Sí, es un hombre.   _No, no son unos muchachos._

                                  Es una muchacha.

1. ¿Es una bebé?   2. ¿Son unas mujeres?

_____   _____

_____   _____

3. ¿Es un joven?   4. ¿Es una muchacha?

_____   _____

_____   _____

5. ¿Es un bebé?

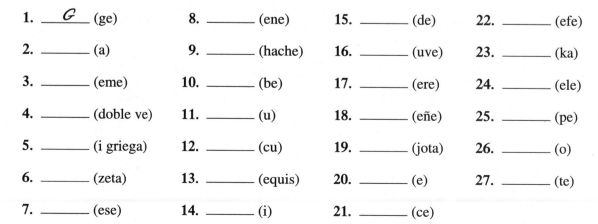

6. ¿Son unos amigos?

_____

_____

_____

_____

D. A PG-13 movie has just opened at the local theater. Make a list of the people who can attend and those who cannot. Use plural forms.

PUEDEN ASISTIR *(CAN ATTEND)*	NO PUEDEN ASISTIR *(CANNOT ATTEND)*
los hombres	*los bebés*
_____	_____
_____	_____

VOCABULARIO   Las letras del alfabeto español *Letters of the Spanish alphabet*

E. Here are the names of the Spanish letters. Write the letter for each in the space provided. The first one has been done for you.

1. __*G*__ (ge)   **8.** _____ (ene)   **15.** _____ (de)   **22.** _____ (efe)

2. _____ (a)   **9.** _____ (hache)   **16.** _____ (uve)   **23.** _____ (ka)

3. _____ (eme)   **10.** _____ (be)   **17.** _____ (ere)   **24.** _____ (ele)

4. _____ (doble ve)   **11.** _____ (u)   **18.** _____ (eñe)   **25.** _____ (pe)

5. _____ (i griega)   **12.** _____ (cu)   **19.** _____ (jota)   **26.** _____ (o)

6. _____ (zeta)   **13.** _____ (equis)   **20.** _____ (e)   **27.** _____ (te)

7. _____ (ese)   **14.** _____ (i)   **21.** _____ (ce)

CONVERSACIÓN *Asking about spelling, Asking about names*

F. Write a conversation in which Alicia and Bernardo meet for the first time.

ALICIA *(greeting)* _____

BERNARDO *(greeting)* _____

ALICIA *(asks name)* _____

BERNARDO *(tells first name)* _____

ALICIA *(asks last name)* _____

BERNARDO *(tells last name)* _____

ALICIA *(asks how to spell last name)* _____

BERNARDO *(tells how to spell)* _____

    (asks Alicia's name) _____

ALICIA *(tells full name)* _____

BERNARDO *(says pleased to meet)* _____

ALICIA *(says pleased also)* _____

BERNARDO *(says good-bye)* _____

ALICIA *(says until meet again)* _____

G. Write the conversation in which Alicia introduces Bernardo to Carlota. Use expressions from Lesson 1 and Lesson 2.

ALICIA *(greets Bernardo)* _____

BERNARDO *(returns greeting)* _____

    (asks Alicia who other girl is) _____

ALICIA *(says the girl's name is Carlota)* _____

    (introduces Carlota to Bernardo) _____

BERNARDO *(says he's happy to meet her)* _____

    CARLOTA *(says she's happy also)* _____

    ALICIA *(says good-bye)* _____

    BERNARDO, CARLOTA *(say they will see her tomorrow)* _____

H. Eleonor Gutiérrez Mendoza married Raúl García Ibarra.

   1. What is her name after marriage?

     _____

   2. What is his name after marriage?

     _____

   3. They name their son Esteban. What is his full name?

     _____

   4. They name their daughter Julia. What is her full name?

     _____

   5. What is Julia's name after she marries José García Silva?

     _____

Nombre _____

✦ Unidad I Lección 3 ✦

La familia, los números, la edad
The family, numbers, age

VOCABULARIO   La familia *The family*

A. Fill in each blank with the word that tells the relationship between the two people. Use the family tree.

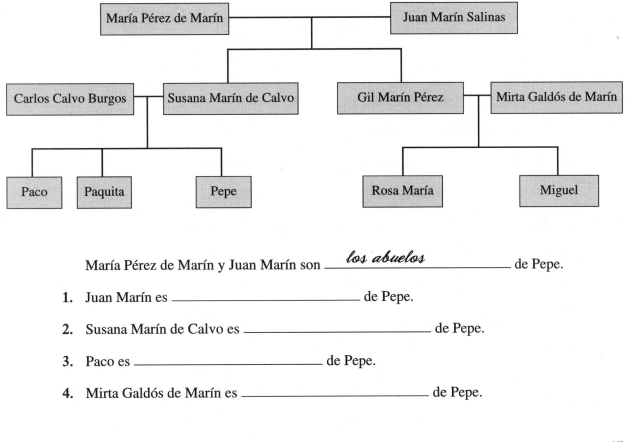

María Pérez de Marín y Juan Marín son ___*los abuelos*___ de Pepe.

1. Juan Marín es _____ de Pepe.

2. Susana Marín de Calvo es _____ de Pepe.

3. Paco es _____ de Pepe.

4. Mirta Galdós de Marín es _____ de Pepe.

5. Miguel es _____ de Pepe.

6. Carlos Calvo y Susana Marín son _____ de Pepe.

7. Carlos Calvo es _____ de Pepe.

8. Gil Marín y Mirta Galdós de Marín son _____ de Pepe.

9. Rosa María es _____ de Pepe.

10. Paquita es _____ de Pepe.

11. María Pérez de Marín es _____ de Pepe.

12. Paquita es _____ de Carlos y Susana de Calvo.

13. Pepe y Paco son _____ de Juan Marín y María Pérez de Marín.

B. Tell how the following people are related to you.

El padre de mi padre es mi _____*abuelo*_____ .

1. La hija de mi tío es mi _____ .

2. La hermana de mi madre es mi _____ .

3. La esposa de mi padre es mi _____ .

4. Mi abuela es la _____ de mi madre.

5. Mi primo es el _____ de mi tío.

6. Mi hermano es el _____ de mi padre.

7. El hermano de mi prima es mi _____ .

8. El hermano de mi abuelo es el _____ de mi padre.

9. El esposo de mi tía es el _____ de mi primo.

CONVERSACIÓN   *Telling where someone is*

C. La familia Gómez   Look at the members of the Gómez family and tell where they are. Use the verb **estar** and the words for *here* and *there*.

¿Dónde está el padre? _____*El padre está aquí.*_____

1. ¿Dónde está la madre? _____

2. ¿Dónde están las nietas? _____

3. ¿Dónde está la bebé? _____

4. ¿Dónde están los abuelos? _____

5. ¿Dónde está el hijo? _____

6. ¿Dónde están las hermanas? _____

7. ¿Dónde está la abuela? _____

8. ¿Dónde está el hermano? _____

D. Write the name and relationship of six people who are important to you in the spaces under the circles. If you wish, use the circles to draw a picture of each person.

"Circle of People Who Are Important to Me"

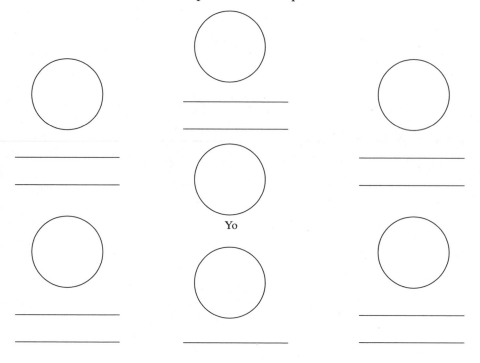

E. Write complete sentences to tell where the following people are. Use the appropriate form of **estar** with these expressions: **en casa, en la escuela,** or **en el trabajo.**

mi padre _____ *Mi padre está en casa.* _____

1. tus abuelos _____

2. tu madre _____

3. tus primos _____

4. tu hermano o hermana _____

5. tu tío _____

6. tu tía _____

7. _____

8. _____

9. _____

10. _____

VOCABULARIO   Los números *Numbers*

F. Write the following amounts in words.

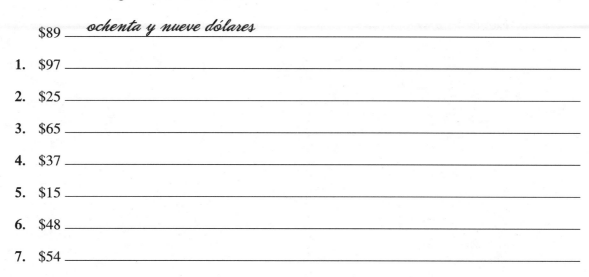

$89 *ochenta y nueve dólares*_____

1. $97 _____

2. $25 _____

3. $65 _____

4. $37 _____

5. $15 _____

6. $48 _____

7. $54 _____

VOCABULARIO   Las funciones aritméticas *Arithmetic functions*

G. Calculaciones   Write these arithmetic problems in words.

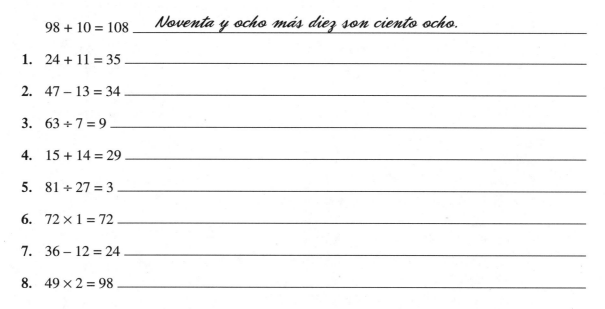

98 + 10 = 108 *Noventa y ocho más diez son ciento ocho.*_____

1. 24 + 11 = 35 _____

2. 47 – 13 = 34 _____

3. 63 ÷ 7 = 9 _____

4. 15 + 14 = 29 _____

5. 81 ÷ 27 = 3 _____

6. 72 × 1 = 72 _____

7. 36 – 12 = 24 _____

8. 49 × 2 = 98 _____

CONVERSACIÓN *Asking and telling how many there are*

H. Look at the pictures and tell how many objects there are.

estrellas *(stars)*

Hay cuarenta y nueve estrellas.

1. árboles *(trees)*

2. manzanas *(apples)*

3. tiendas de acampar *(tents)*

4. peces *(fish)*

5. flores *(flowers)*

6. botones *(buttons)*

7. diamantes *(diamonds)*

I. Comparing four items in Activity H, write whether there are more than, less than, or as many as.

Hay más manzanas que botones.

1. _____

2. _____

3. _____

4. _____

CONVERSACIÓN *Asking and telling about age*

J. The following people are celebrating their birthdays today. Ask them how old they are. Write your question on the first line. Use formal or informal questions according to the person you are asking. On the second line, write their answer to your question.

Enrique/17

¿Cuántos años tienes, Enrique?

Tengo diez y siete años.

1. Señora García / 32

_____

_____

2. Marilú / 5

_____

_____

3. Señor Marín / 48

_____

_____

4. Pablo / 14

_____

_____

5. Señorita Flores / 21

_____

_____

K. Tell how old each of the people in Activity J is.

Enrique *tiene diez y siete años.*

1. La señora García _____ .

2. Marilú _____ .

3. El señor Marín _____ .

4. Pablo _____ .

5. La señorita Flores _____ .

L. Make a list of people you know and tell their ages.

Mi madre tiene treinta y cinco años.

1. _____

2. _____

3. _____

4. _____

5. _____

DIVERSIÓN

Letras mezcladas   Unscramble the letters to tell the member of the family.

aerdp   *padre* _____

1. damer _____

2. lbeoua _____

3. ramehan _____

4. mrpoi _____

5. ajih _____

6. ssooep _____

7. íat _____

8. teion _____

Nombre _____

⇒ Unidad I Lección 4 ⇐

El cuerpo y las enfermedades
The body and illnesses

VOCABULARIO   El cuerpo   *The body*

A. Identify the parts of the body.

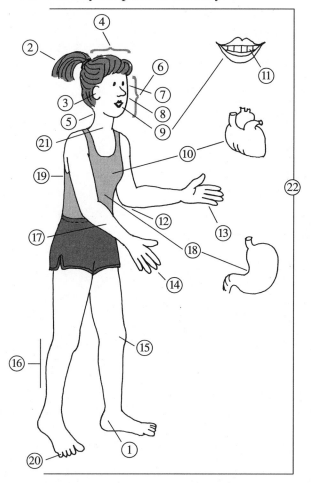

1. _____ 12. _____

2. _____ 13. _____

3. _____ 14. _____

4. _____ 15. _____

5. _____ 16. _____

6. _____ 17. _____

7. _____ 18. _____

8. _____ 19. _____

9. _____ 20. _____

10. _____ 21. _____

11. _____ 22. _____

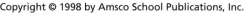

B. What part of the body does each of the following describe?

I see with these. ___*los ojos*_____

1. I hear with these. _____

2. I walk on these. _____

3. I eat with these. _____

4. I raise this to answer a question. _____

5. I comb this. _____

6. I wash these. _____

7. This hurts when I'm sick. _____

8. I draw this to say "I love you." _____

9. I use these when I have an itch. _____

CONVERSACIÓN *Asking and telling what something is*

C. **¿Qué es esto?** In a complete sentence, identify each of the following parts of the body.

1. _____

2. _____

3. _____

4. _____

5. _____

6. _____

7. _____

8. _____

9. _____

10. _____

Nombre _____

CONVERSACIÓN *Talking more about health*

D. **¿Qué tienen estas personas?**   For each drawing write what Dr. Rodríguez might say to inquire about the person's health. Give the person's response.

DR. RODRÍGUEZ _¿Cómo está Ud.?_____

LA MUJER _Tengo la gripe._____

1. DR. RODRÍGUEZ _____

   EL HOMBRE _____

2. DR. RODRÍGUEZ _____

   EL NIÑO _____

3. DR. RODRÍGUEZ _____

   LA MUJER _____

4. DR. RODRÍGUEZ _____

   EL HOMBRE _____

5. DR. RODRÍGUEZ _____

   LA NIÑA _____

6. DR. RODRÍGUEZ _____

   EL HOMBRE _____

Compañeros, Spanish for Communication, Book 1
Cuaderno de actividades

E. **¿Qué le duele?** *What hurts?* Tell what's hurting each member of the soccer team. They can be identified by the number on their shirt.

Le duele el cuello. _____

1. _____

2. _____

3. _____

4. _____

5. _____

6. _____

7. _____

8. _____

9. _____

F. Rewrite the following conversation in Spanish. The first line is done for you.

JUAN   (1) Hi, María.
MARÍA   (2) Hi, Juan. How are you?
JUAN   (3) Not well. I have a cold and I have a fever.
MARÍA   (4) What hurts you?
JUAN   (5) I have a headache and my throat hurts.
MARÍA   (6) That's too bad. *(Juan sneezes.)* Bless you.
JUAN   (7) Thank you. And you, María, how are you?
MARÍA   (8) I'm well, thank you.
JUAN   (9) You're welcome.
MARÍA   (10) See you tomorrow?
JUAN   (11) Yes, see you later.
MARÍA   (12) Good-bye.

1. *Hola, María.*
2. _____
3. _____
4. _____
5. _____
6. _____
7. _____
8. _____
9. _____
10. _____
11. _____
12. _____

DIVERSIÓN

Recipe for a monster On a separate sheet of paper, draw a monster with the following body parts.

un cuerpo grande	cuatro orejas	cuatro piernas
dos cuellos	ocho dientes	cuatro pies
dos cabezas	dos brazos	siete dedos en cada pie
seis ojos	dos manos	dos corazones
dos narices	ocho dedos	mucho pelo
cuatro bocas		

Nombre _____

⟫ Unidad I Lección 5 ⟪

La ropa y el tiempo
Clothing and weather

VOCABULARIO   **La ropa** *Clothing*

A. *Let's take a trip.*   Decide on a destination and then make a list of some of the clothing you will take with you.

     Destinación _____

       unos zapatos _____

1. _____ 4. _____

2. _____ 5. _____

3. _____ 6. _____

CONVERSACIÓN   *Asking what something is*

B. **¿Qué es eso?**   Answer in a complete sentence to say *That is a . . .* or *Those are some . . .*

          Ésos son unos calcetines. _____

1. _____

2. _____

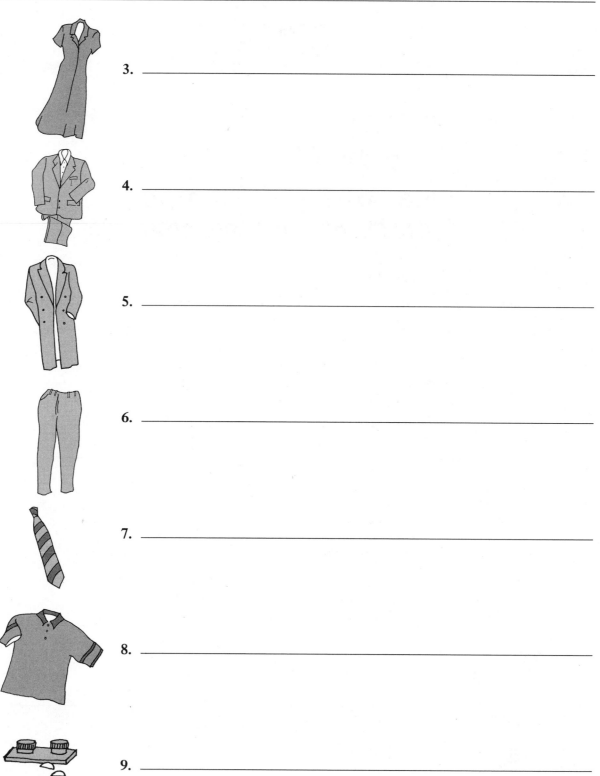

3. _____

4. _____

5. _____

6. _____

7. _____

8. _____

9. _____

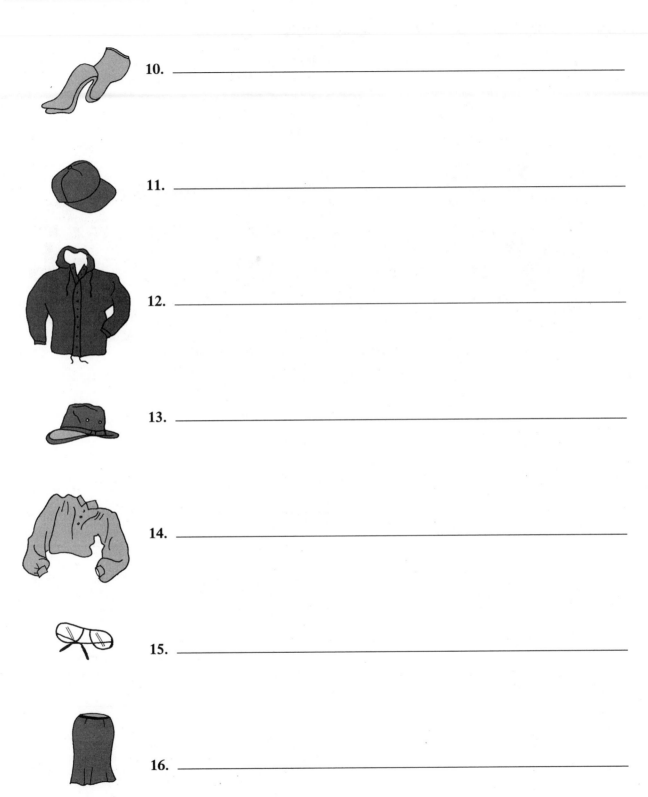

10. _____

11. _____

12. _____

13. _____

14. _____

15. _____

16. _____

CONVERSACIÓN *Telling who something belongs to*

C. **¿De quién es?** Juan is sorting out the laundry for himself, his brother Roberto who is in the room with him, and his sister Susana. Help him tell his brother *That . . . is mine/yours/hers.*

Ese suéter es tuyo.

1. _____

2. _____

3. _____

4. _____

5. _____

6. _____

7. _____

8. _____

9. _____

10. _____

CONVERSACIÓN *Talking about what one is wearing*

D. **¿Qué llevas?**   Help Carlos and Julia answer the question *What are you wearing?*

CARLOS   Yo llevo _____

_____

_____ .

JULIA   Y yo llevo _____

_____

_____ .

E. **Te toca a ti.** *It's your turn.*   Tell what you and other people are wearing today.

_____

_____

_____

_____

_____

_____

VOCABULARIO   El tiempo *The weather*

F.   **¿Qué tiempo hace?**   Tell what the weather is like in these pictures.

Hace sol. Hace calor.

1. _____

2. _____

3. _____

4. _____

5. _____

G. **¿Qué tiempo hace en… ?** Use the weather map to tell what the weather is like in different cities.

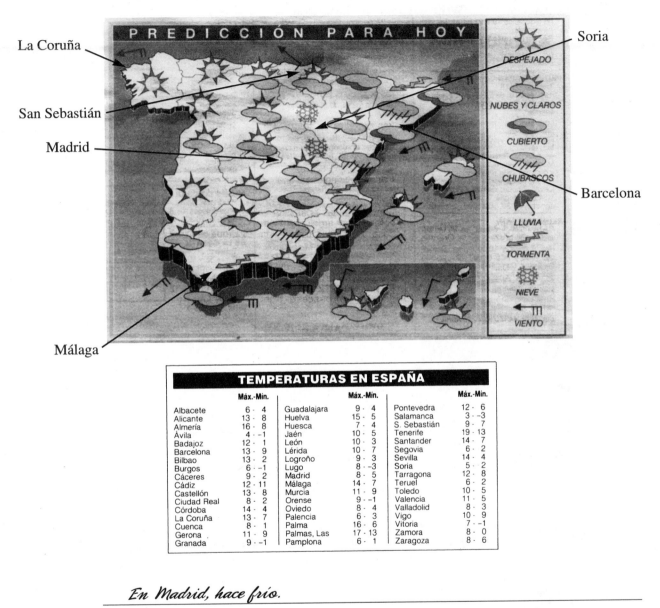

En Madrid, hace frío.

1. _____

2. _____

3. _____

4. _____

5. _____

VOCABULARIO La estación *The season*

H. **¿Qué estación es?** Write the name of the season.

1. _____

2. _____

3. _____

4. _____

I. **¿Qué llevas cuando… ?** *What do you wear when . . . ?* First name the article of clothing in the drawing, then using **lo/la/los/las** describe what the weather is like when you wear it/them.

la chaqueta

La llevo cuando hace fresco.

1. _____

_____

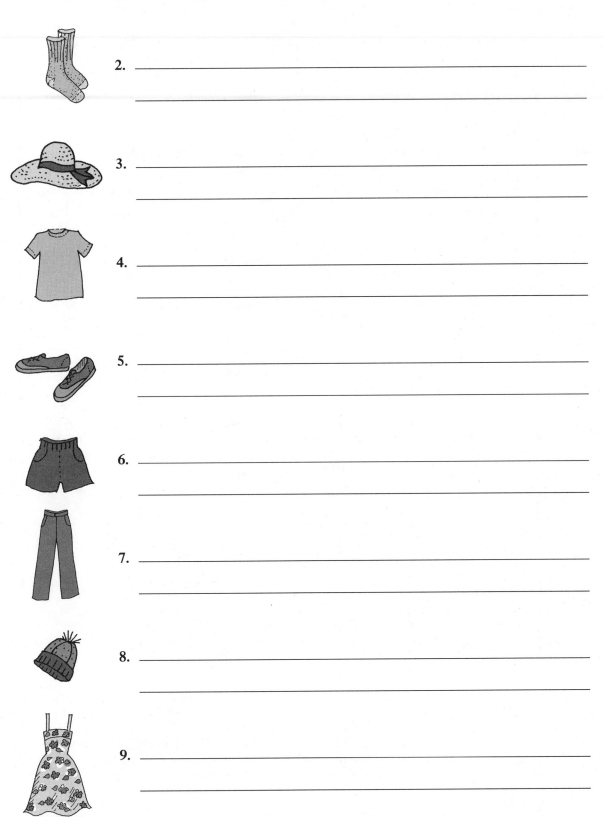

2. _____

_____

3. _____

_____

4. _____

_____

5. _____

_____

6. _____

_____

7. _____

_____

8. _____

_____

9. _____

_____

DIVERSIÓN

¿Qué llevan?   Here is a fashion show of your latest fashion designs!
Draw the clothing that each person is wearing.

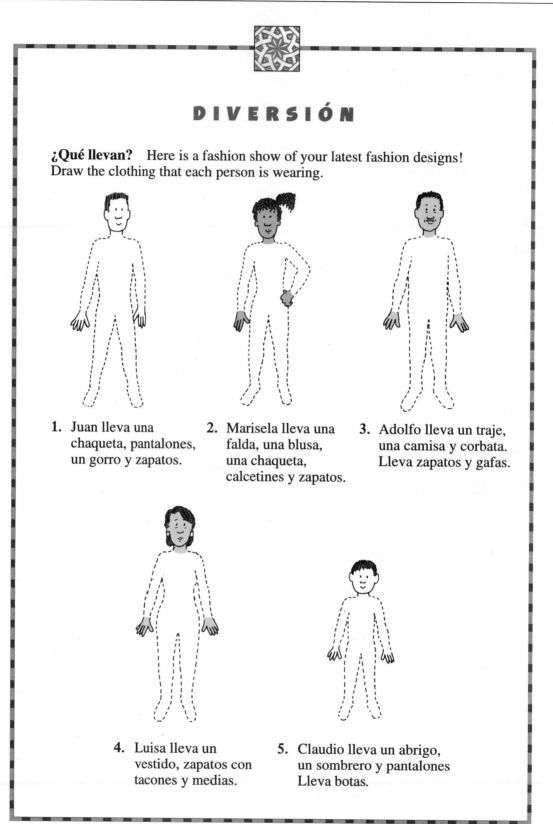

1. Juan lleva una chaqueta, pantalones, un gorro y zapatos.

2. Marisela lleva una falda, una blusa, una chaqueta, calcetines y zapatos.

3. Adolfo lleva un traje, una camisa y corbata. Lleva zapatos y gafas.

4. Luisa lleva un vestido, zapatos con tacones y medias.

5. Claudio lleva un abrigo, un sombrero y pantalones Lleva botas.

➤ Unidad I Lección 6 ➤

La comida y los animales
Food and animals

VOCABULARIO   La comida *Food*

A. ¿Qué es esto?   Name the food in a complete sentence saying *this is/these are*. Follow the model.

Ésta es lechuga. _____

1. _____

2. _____

3. _____

4. _____

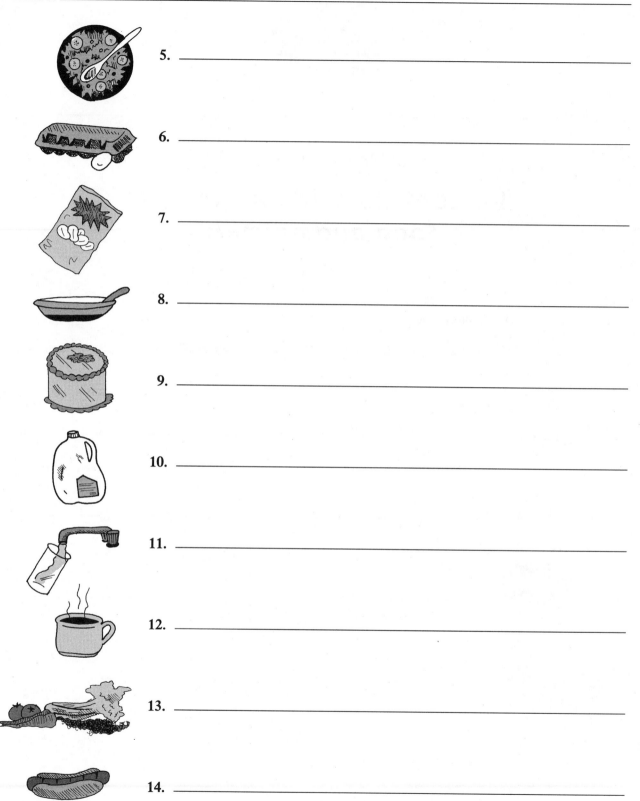

5. _____

6. _____

7. _____

8. _____

9. _____

10. _____

11. _____

12. _____

13. _____

14. _____

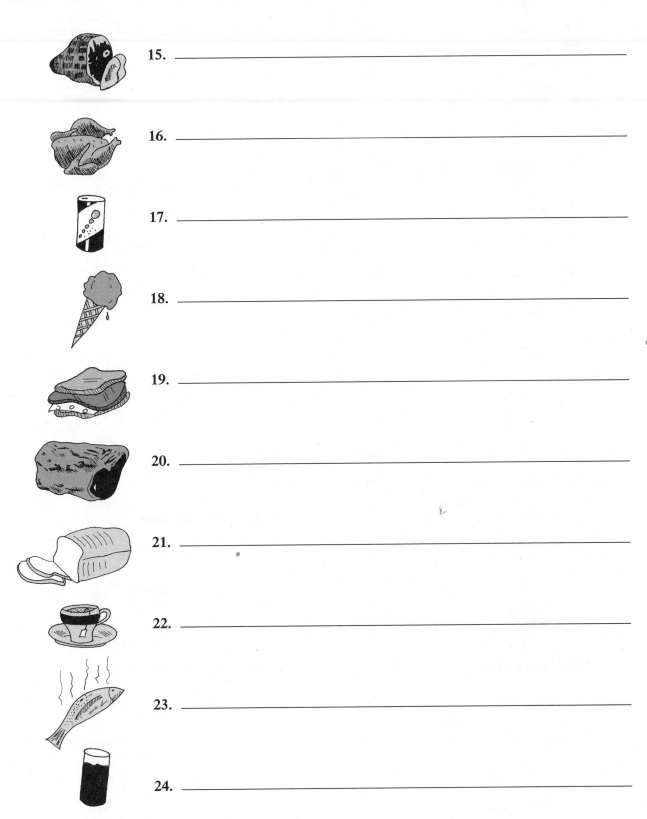

15. _____

16. _____

17. _____

18. _____

19. _____

20. _____

21. _____

22. _____

23. _____

24. _____

B. *You're the cook!* Combine the following to prepare different kinds of salads, sandwiches, and soups.

ensalada	papas	lechuga
sándwich	frutas	legumbres
sopa	rosbif	huevos
	pollo	jamón

una ensalada de lechuga _____

1. _____

2. _____

3. _____

4. _____

5. _____

6. _____

CONVERSACIÓN *Talking about what one eats and drinks*

C. Make a list of the foods you eat at each of these meals.

1. **Para el desayuno, como...**

_____

_____

_____

2. **Para el almuerzo, como...**

_____

_____

_____

3. **Para la cena, como...**

_____

_____

_____

4. **Para la merienda, como...**

_____

_____

_____

D. Tell when you eat the following.

¿Cuándo comes las hamburguesas? ___*Como las hamburguesas para el almuerzo.*___

¿Cuándo come tu familia el rosbif? ___*Comemos el rosbif para la cena.*___

1. ¿Cuándo comen Uds. las papas? _____

2. ¿Cuándo comes los huevos? _____

3. ¿Cuándo comes las perros calientes? _____

4. ¿Cuándo comes las papas fritas? _____

5. ¿Cuándo comen tus primos el helado? _____

6. ¿Cuándo come tu madre la ensalada? _____

7. ¿Cuándo come tu familia el pollo? _____

8. ¿Cuándo comen Uds. el pescado? _____

9. ¿Cuándo comen tus amigos la sopa? _____

10. ¿Cuándo comen Uds. el jamón? _____

11. ¿Cuándo comes las tortas? _____

12. ¿Cuándo comes los sándwiches? _____

13. ¿Cuándo comen tus amigos las frutas? _____

14. ¿Cuándo come tu familia el pan? _____

15. ¿Cuándo comes las legumbres? _____

16. ¿Cuándo comen tú y tus amigos las papitas fritas? _____

17. ¿Cuándo comes la lechuga? _____

18. ¿Cuándo bebes la leche? _____

19. ¿Cuándo bebe tu padre el café? _____

20. ¿Cuándo bebes el agua? _____

21. ¿Cuándo beben Uds. un refresco? _____

22. ¿Cuándo bebe tu abuela el té? _____

CONVERSACIÓN   *Telling what one likes and dislikes*

E. Make a list of the foods you like and another list of those you do not like.

ME GUSTA(N)   NO ME GUSTA(N)

_____   _____

_____   _____

_____   _____

_____   _____

_____   _____

_____   _____

F. Think of people you know and tell a food that each likes and a food that each dislikes.

A mi madre le gusta la ensalada. No le gusta el jamón.

A mi padre le gustan los sándwiches. No le gustan las frutas.

1. _____

2. _____

3. _____

4. _____

5. _____

6. _____

VOCABULARIO   Los animales *Animals*

G. **¿Qué es eso?**   Describe each picture with a complete sentence.

Éste es un tigre.

1. _____

2. _____

3. _____

4. _____

5. _____

6. _____

7. _____

8. _____

9. _____

10. _____

11. _____

12. _____

13. _____

14. _____

15. _____

16. _____

17. _____

18. _____

19. _____

20. _____

21. _____

H. Make three lists

WILD ANIMALS	FARM/RANCH ANIMALS	ANIMALS KEPT AS PETS
_____	_____	_____
_____	_____	_____
_____	_____	_____
_____	_____	_____

DIVERSIÓN

A. The animals have escaped from the zoo. Can you help the zookeeper find all the animals? Draw a line from the animal's nameplate to the animal.

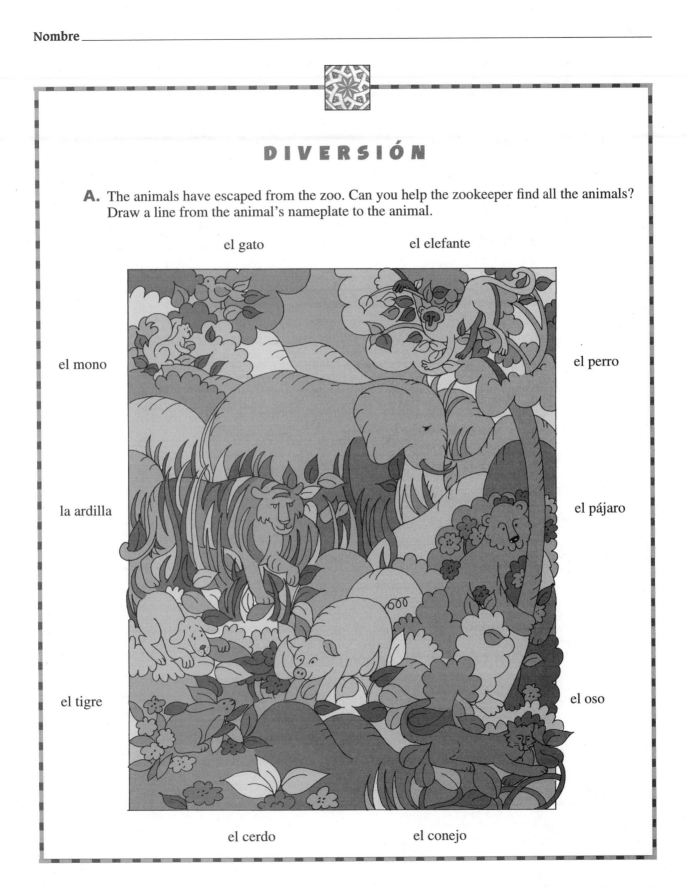

el gato   el elefante

el mono   el perro

la ardilla   el pájaro

el tigre   el oso

el cerdo   el conejo

B. The grocery bag broke and all the food spilled out and got mixed up. Sort out the food and then circle your favorites.

E E C H L *LECHE*

1. H L D O A E _____

2. A S P O _____

3. O S R E R F E C _____

4. L L O P O _____

5. A Ó N J M _____

6. F A I P R S P T S A A _____

7. O B F R S I _____

8. A A P P _____

9. T R S A U F _____

10. L N A D E A A S _____

11. A U G B H U R M S E A _____

12. U V H O E _____

13. O R T A T _____

14. C E D O A P S _____

15. U A G A _____

16. É A F C _____

17. R U E L G M S E B _____

18. Á S D N I W C H _____

19. U E G C H A L _____

Nombre _____

⋙ Unidad I Lección 7 ⋘

La casa, los colores, las formas y los tamaños
The house, colors, shapes, and sizes

VOCABULARIO   **La casa y el apartamento** *The house and the apartment*

A. Identify the parts of the house and list them on the next page.

Nombre _____

1. _____	8. _____
2. _____	9. _____
3. _____	10. _____
4. _____	11. _____
5. _____	12. _____
6. _____	13. _____
7. _____	14. _____

B. In Spanish, name the room where you do the following.

eat breakfast ___*la cocina*_____

1. sleep _____
2. brush teeth _____
3. watch television _____
4. wash clothes _____
5. hang clothes _____
6. talk on the telephone _____
7. store unused things _____
8. take a bath _____
9. entertain friends _____
10. cook dinner _____
11. do homework _____
12. barbecue _____
13. play ball _____
14. pass through to go to another room _____

VOCABULARIO Los colores *Colors*

C. Name three objects that are each of the following colors. How many things can you name in Spanish?

1. rojo(a)

   _____

   _____

   _____

2. azul

   _____

   _____

   _____

3. anaranjado(a)

   _____

   _____

   _____

4. verde

   _____

   _____

   _____

5. morado(a)

   _____

   _____

   _____

6. violeta

   _____

   _____

   _____

7. amarillo(a)

   _____

   _____

   _____

8. negro(a)

   _____

   _____

   _____

9. blanco(a)

   _____

   _____

   _____

10. gris

   _____

   _____

   _____

11. pardo(a)

   _____

   _____

   _____

12. rosado(a)

   _____

   _____

   _____

VOCABULARIO   Las formas y los tamaños *Shapes and sizes*

D. Name two objects that are each of the following shapes and sizes.

1. grande

    _____

    _____

2. pequeño(a)

    _____

    _____

3. mediano(a)

    _____

    _____

4. ancho(a)

    _____

    _____

5. estrecho(a)

    _____

    _____

6. cuadrado(a)

    _____

    _____

7. alto(a)

    _____

    _____

8. bajo(a)

    _____

    _____

9. largo(a)

    _____

    _____

10. corto(a)

    _____

    _____

11. redondo(a)

    _____

    _____

12. plano(a)

    _____

    _____

CONVERSACIÓN   *Describing things*

E. Describe what you are wearing today. Tell as much as you can about each item (color, size, shape, etc.).

Yo llevo una camisa. Mi camisa es azul.

F. Describe these things. Tell the following about each: **¿De qué color es? ¿De qué forma es? ¿De qué tamaño es?**

1. _____

_____

_____

2. _____

_____

_____

3. _____

_____

_____

4. _____

_____

_____

5. _____

_____

_____

6. _____

_____

_____

7. _____

8. _____

9. _____

10. _____

11. _____

12. _____

CONVERSACIÓN *Comparing things*

G. Compare the following objects in shape or size.

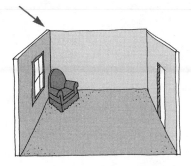

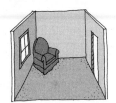

Este cuarto es más grande.

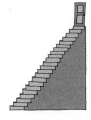

1. _____

2. _____

3. _____

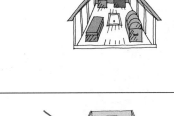

4. _____

H. *Compare again!*   Can you make some comparisons of these very different objects?

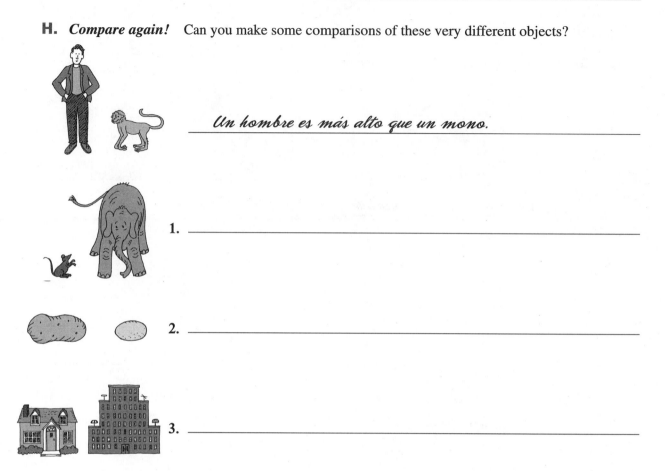

Un hombre es más alto que un mono.
_____

1. _____

2. _____

3. _____

CONVERSACIÓN   *Talking about where someone lives, Describing things*

I. Describe what kind of a place you and other people you know live in. Be sure to use the correct form of **vivir.**

Nosotros vivimos en un apartamento alto. Es verde y gris.
_____

1. _____

2. _____

3. _____

4. _____

5. _____

6. _____

CONVERSACIÓN *Telling where things are*

J. Tell on what floor in your home the following rooms are.

1. tu alcoba _____

2. los baños _____

3. la sala de estar _____

4. el comedor _____

5. el desván _____

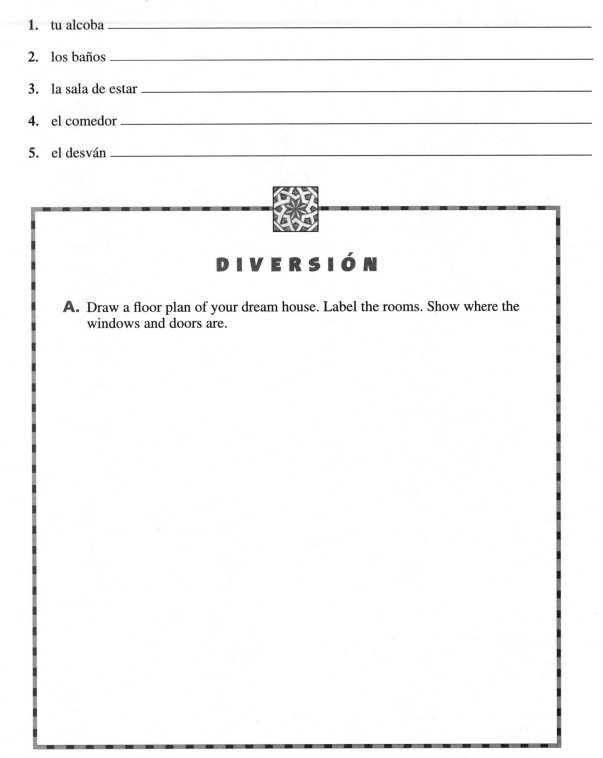

DIVERSIÓN

A. Draw a floor plan of your dream house. Label the rooms. Show where the windows and doors are.

B. Find the country on the map and color it using the designated color

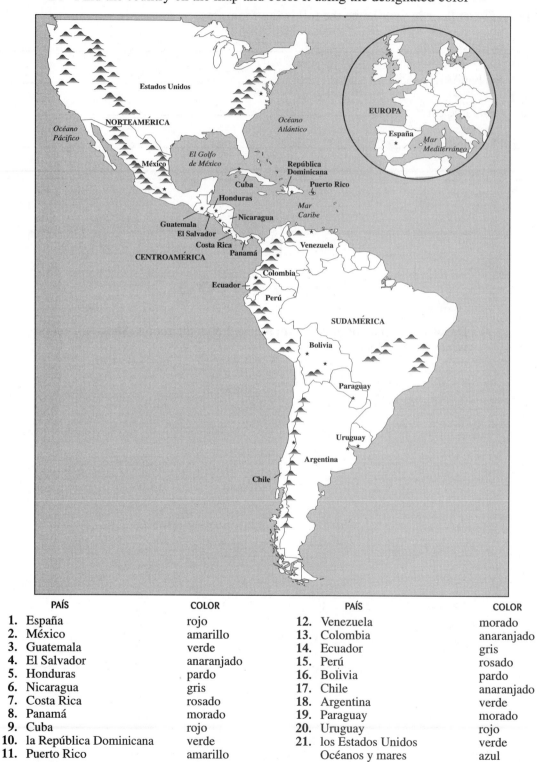

	PAÍS	COLOR		PAÍS	COLOR
1.	España	rojo	12.	Venezuela	morado
2.	México	amarillo	13.	Colombia	anaranjado
3.	Guatemala	verde	14.	Ecuador	gris
4.	El Salvador	anaranjado	15.	Perú	rosado
5.	Honduras	pardo	16.	Bolivia	pardo
6.	Nicaragua	gris	17.	Chile	anaranjado
7.	Costa Rica	rosado	18.	Argentina	verde
8.	Panamá	morado	19.	Paraguay	morado
9.	Cuba	rojo	20.	Uruguay	rojo
10.	la República Dominicana	verde	21.	los Estados Unidos	verde
11.	Puerto Rico	amarillo		Océanos y mares	azul

Nombre _____

❧ Unidad I Lección 8 ❧

Las cosas en el aula y otras cosas
Things in the classroom and other things

VOCABULARIO   **Las cosas en el aula** *Things in the classroom*

A. Identify the following.

1. _____	4. _____
2. _____	5. _____
3. _____	6. _____

7. _____   18. _____

8. _____   19. _____

9. _____   20. _____

10. _____   21. _____

11. _____   22. _____

12. _____   23. _____

13. _____   24. _____

14. _____   25. _____

15. _____   26. _____

16. _____   27. _____

17. _____   28. _____

B. Make a list of items that belong to each of the following categories.

1. Objects on classroom wall(s)   4. Classroom furniture

   _____   _____

   _____   _____

   _____   _____

2. Objects used for writing   5. Things one can read

   _____   _____

   _____   _____

   _____   _____

3. Objects used for storage   6. Miscellaneous objects

   _____   _____

   _____   _____

   _____   _____

VOCABULARIO   Otras cosas *Other things*

C. Identify the following.

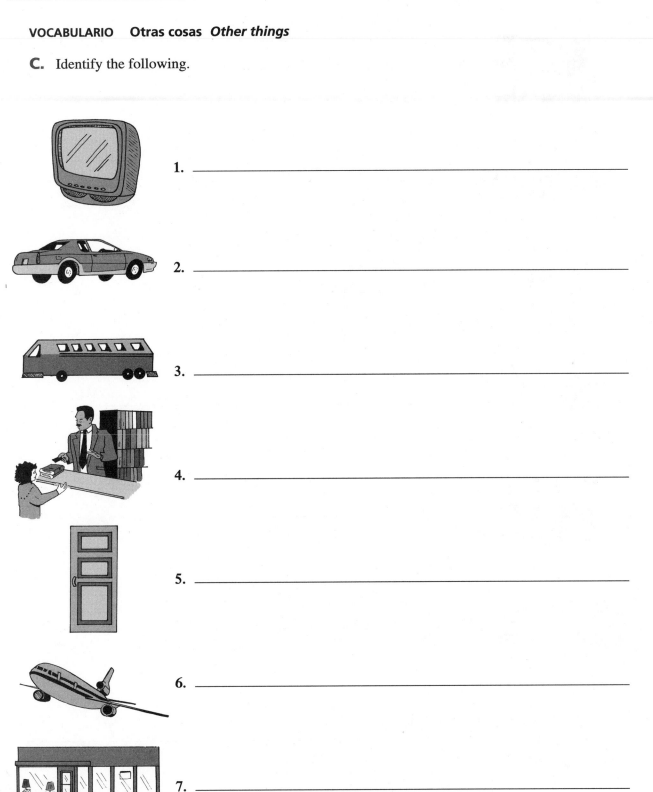

1. _____

2. _____

3. _____

4. _____

5. _____

6. _____

7. _____

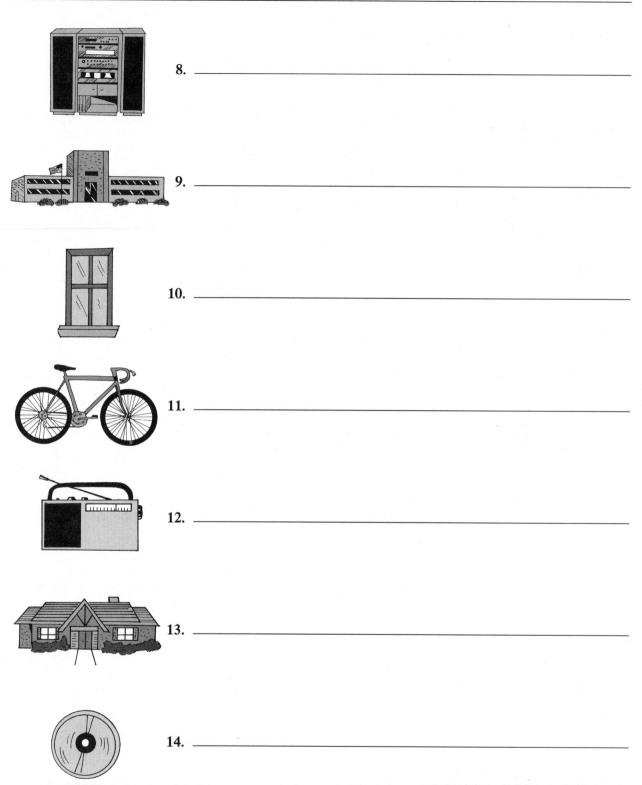

8. _____

9. _____

10. _____

11. _____

12. _____

13. _____

14. _____

15. _____

16. _____

D. Explain in English what these groups of objects have in common.

1. el radio, el televisor, el estéreo, el disco _____

2. el coche, el avión, el autobús, la bicicleta _____

3. la carta, el teléfono _____

4. la escuela, la casa _____

5. la mesa, la silla _____

6. la puerta, la ventana _____

7. un libro, una carta, un cuaderno _____

8. un borrador, una goma, una cesta _____

E. Review the describing words from Lesson 7. Then tell two things that describe each of the following items.

1. tu televisor _____

2. tu libro de español _____

3. tu coche _____

4. la bandera americana _____

5. el aula _____

6. la escuela _____

7. tu casa _____

F. Make a list of five items that you have and another list of five things you do not have. Describe the things you have.

TENGO...   NO TENGO...

un coche verde   _bolígrafos_

1. _____   _____

2. _____   _____

3. _____   _____

4. _____   _____

5. _____   _____

CONVERSACIÓN   *Telling where one is going*

G. Make a list of seven places you and people you know go. Tell how they go there. Be sure to use the correct form of the verb **ir.**

Yo _*Voy a Prince Burger.   Voy en coche.*_

1. Mis amigos _____

2. Mi madre _____

3. Mis abuelos _____

4. Mi amigo y yo _____

5. Mi familia _____

6. El presidente _____

7. Un perro _____

DIVERSIÓN

On a separate sheet of paper, draw a diagram of your classroom and label the things in it.

❧ Unidad I Lección 9 ❧

El calendario, la hora y las clases
The calendar, time, and classes

VOCABULARIO **El calendario** *The calendar*

A. First unscramble the days of the week, then put them in order by writing the number.

_____ el sveeju _____   _____ el nmiogdo _____

_____ el daásbo _____   _____ el neuls _____

_____ el saterm _____   _____ el reinevs _____

_____ el cmrlseoié _____

B. Find the months in this **buscapalabras.** Write them in order. The words go forward, backward, and up and down diagonally.

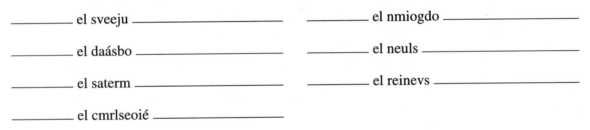

_____   _____

_____   _____

_____   _____

_____   _____

_____   _____

```
B F I O Z R A M P N
S E P T I E M B R E
V B H B A L O S J N
E R O S O G I Y O I
R E R U I B O R A S
B R E W N L C S B M
U O N H U I J F T A
T A E Z J U L I O O
C E R B M E I C I D
O N O V I E M B R E
```

CONVERSACIÓN *Asking the day, Asking the date*

C. Answer the following questions by writing the day and date.

¿Que día es hoy? ___*Hoy es lunes, el dos de octubre.*___

1. ¿Qué día es mañana? _____

2. ¿Qué día es pasado mañana? _____

3. ¿Qué día fue ayer? _____

4. ¿Qué día fue anteayer? _____

D. Write the dates for these events.

el Día de la Raza ___*el doce de octubre*___

1. el Día de San Valentín _____

2. el Día de la Independencia _____

3. el primer día del año _____

4. el último *(last)* día de clase _____

5. tu cumpleaños *(birthday)* _____

E. Write the following dates in the <u>past tense.</u> Remember that the day comes first, then the month, and finally the year.

3/2/75 ___*Fue el tres de febrero de mil novecientos setenta y cinco.*___

1. 12/10/92 _____

2. 1/5/86 _____

3. 27/1/53 _____

4. 19/8/68 _____

5. 25/12/95 _____

VOCABULARIO La hora *Time*

F. **¿Qué hora es?** Write the following times.

Son las tres.

1. _____

2. _____

3. _____

4. _____

5. _____

6. _____

7. _____

8. _____

9. _____

10. _____

VOCABULARIO Las clases *Classes*

G. Make a list of your classes and tell when each begins and ends.

CLASE	COMIENZA	TERMINA	DÍAS

D I V E R S I Ó N

A. On a separate sheet of paper, make a list of the people in your family and your friends and write the date of their birthdays in Spanish.

PERSONA	EL CUMPLEAÑOS
mi madre	*el 17 de abril*

B. In English, make a list of things you do every day. In Spanish, tell what time you do them. Use a separate sheet of paper.

I wake up	*a las siete y media*

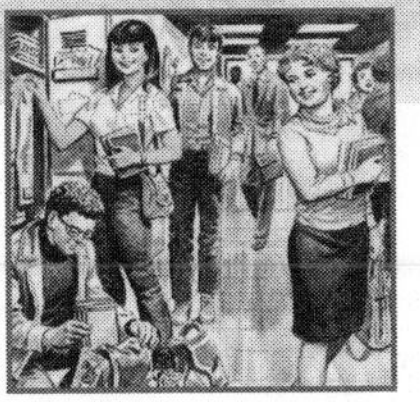

Nombre ______________________________

Unidad I Lección 10

Lo que hacemos y los números grandes
What we do and big numbers

VOCABULARIO Lo que hacemos ***What we do***

A. Tell what the people are doing in each of the following pictures.

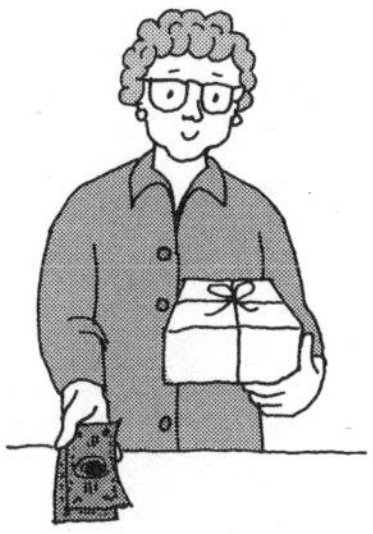

1. ______________________________

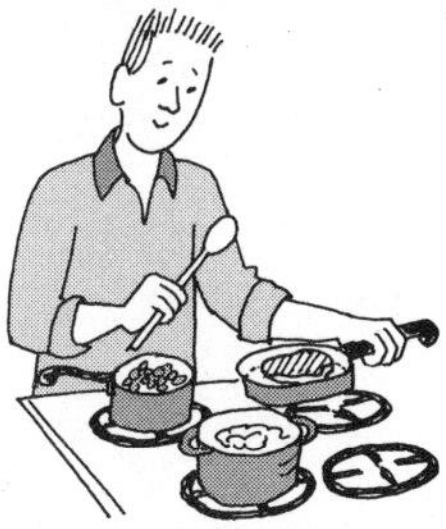

2. ______________________________

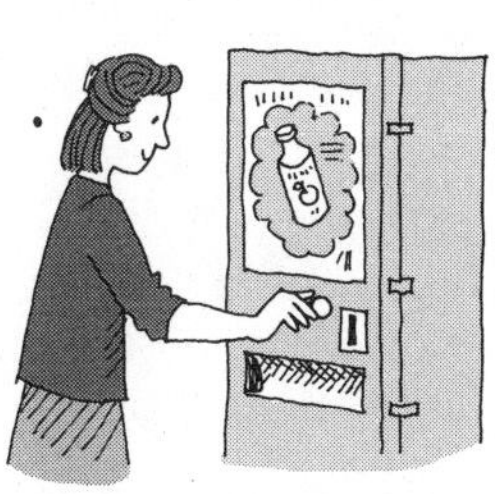

3. ______________________________

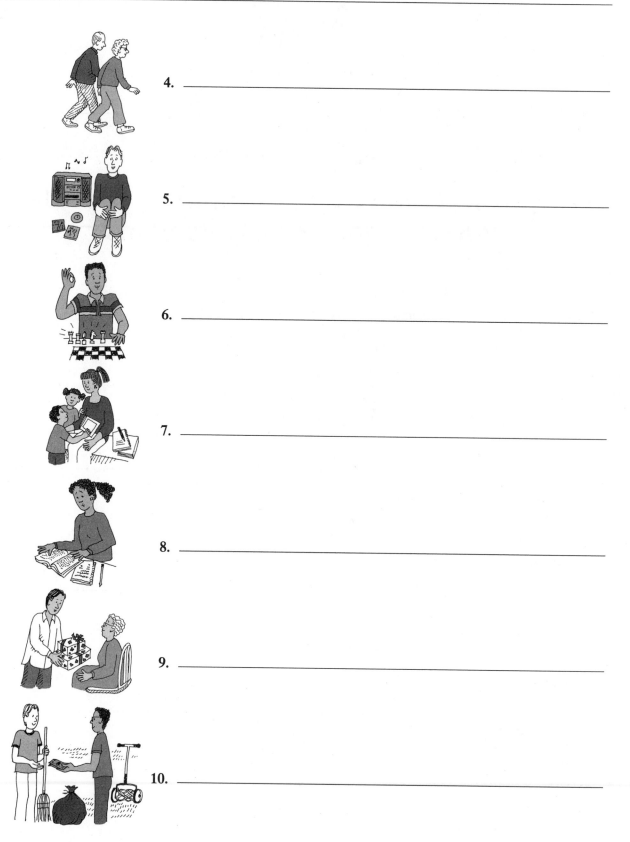

4. _____

5. _____

6. _____

7. _____

8. _____

9. _____

10. _____

11. _____

12. _____

13. _____

14. _____

15. _____

16. _____

17. _____

18. _____

19. _____

20. _____

21. _____

22. _____

23. _____

24. _____

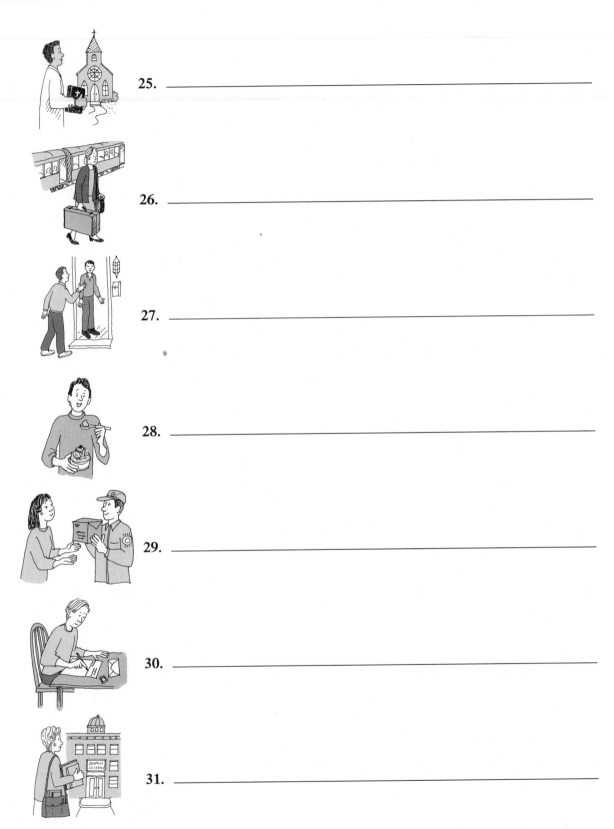

25. _____

26. _____

27. _____

28. _____

29. _____

30. _____

31. _____

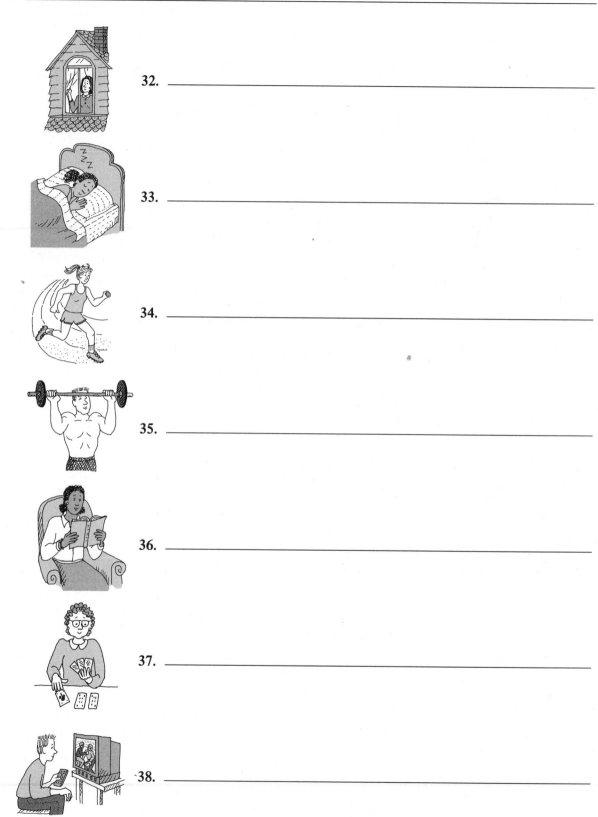

32. _____

33. _____

34. _____

35. _____

36. _____

37. _____

38. _____

B. Using the phrases in Activity A, make a list of things you do often, another list of things you do once in a while, and a third list of things you never do at all.

FRECUENTEMENTE *(OFTEN)*   DE VEZ EN CUANDO *(OCCASIONALLY)*   NUNCA *(NEVER)*

_____   _____   _____

_____   _____   _____

_____   _____   _____

_____   _____   _____

_____   _____   _____

_____   _____   _____

_____   _____   _____

CONVERSACIÓN *Asking and telling what one likes or dislikes doing*

C. Make a list of five things you like to do and five you do not like to do.

ME GUSTA...   NO ME GUSTA...

_____   _____

_____   _____

_____   _____

_____   _____

_____   _____

CONVERSACIÓN *Telling what one is going to do, has to do, and knows how to do*

D. Tell what you have to do and where you are going to do it.

Tengo que estudiar. Voy a estudiar en mi alcoba. _____

1. _____

2. _____

3. _____

4. _____

E. Write some things that you and other people know how to do. Use the appropriate form of **saber.**

Mi padre __*sabe hablar francés.*_____

1. Los estudiantes _____.

2. Mis amigos y yo _____.

3. Yo _____.

4. Mis abuelos _____.

5. Mi profesor(a) _____.

6. Mi amigo(a) _____.

7. Mi madre _____.

8. _____.

9. _____.

10. _____.

CONVERSACIÓN   *Telling what one can and cannot do*

F. Write some things that you and other people can or cannot do. Use the appropriate form of **poder.**

Mi padre __*no puede nadar.*_____

1. Los estudiantes _____.

2. Mis amigos y yo _____.

3. Yo _____.

4. Mis abuelos _____.

5. Mi profesor(a) _____.

6. Mi amigo(a) _____.

7. Mi madre _____.

CONVERSACIÓN   *Telling what one does*

G. Fill in each blank with the appropriate <u>present</u> tense form of the verb. Then write the English equivalent.

Yo (dormir) ___*duermo*___ bien.

___*I sleep well.*___

1. Nosotros (hablar) _____ español un poco.

    _____

2. Los estudiantes (aprender) _____ mucho en la escuela.

    _____

3. Mis amigos (jugar) _____ (al) fútbol.

    _____

4. Los bebés (beber) _____ mucha leche.

    _____

5. ¿(Visitar) _____ tú a tus abuelos frecuentemente?

    _____

6. Mi padre siempre (preparar) _____ la comida.

    _____

7. Nosotros (vivir) _____ en una casa grande.

    _____

8. ¿(Comer) _____ Uds. helado?

    _____

9. Yo (ir) _____ al cine con mis amigos.

    _____

10. La profesora (leer) _____ un libro.

    _____

11. Nosotros (ir) _____ a (ganar) _____ el juego.

_____

12. Yo (dar) _____ muchos regalos.

_____

13. Los perros (correr) _____ en la pista.

_____

14. Mis padres no (tomar) _____ mucho café.

_____

15. Mi familia y yo (jugar) _____ al tenis.

_____

16. ¿(Recibir) _____ Uds. muchas cartas?

_____

17. Sí, nosotros (recibir) _____ muchas cartas.

_____

18. ¿Quién (cocinar) _____ la cena en tu casa?

_____

19. Nosotros siempre (comer) _____ en casa.

_____

20. Me gusta mucho (bailar) _____ en las fiestas.

_____

VOCABULARIO   Los números   *Numbers*

H.   Write the following numbers in numerals.

ochocientos cuarenta y siete   *847* _____

1.   ciento setenta y cuatro _____

2.   quinientos veinte y uno _____

3.   seiscientos cincuenta y seis _____

4.   trescientos noventa y ocho _____

5.   doscientos treinta y cinco _____

6.   setecientos ochenta y dos _____

7.   cuatrocientos sesenta y tres _____

8.   novecientos diez y nueve _____

9.   mil novecientos noventa y nueve _____

I.   Write out the amount in numbers for each of the following items.

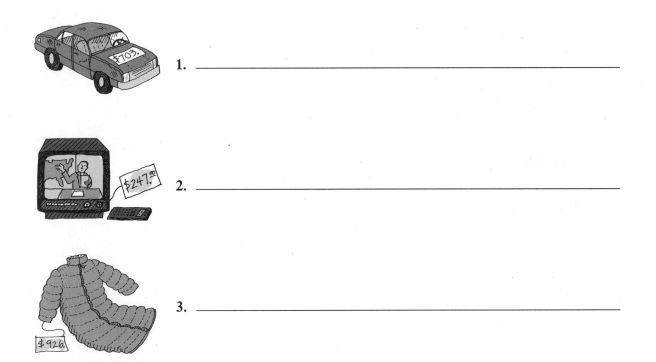

1. _____

2. _____

3. _____

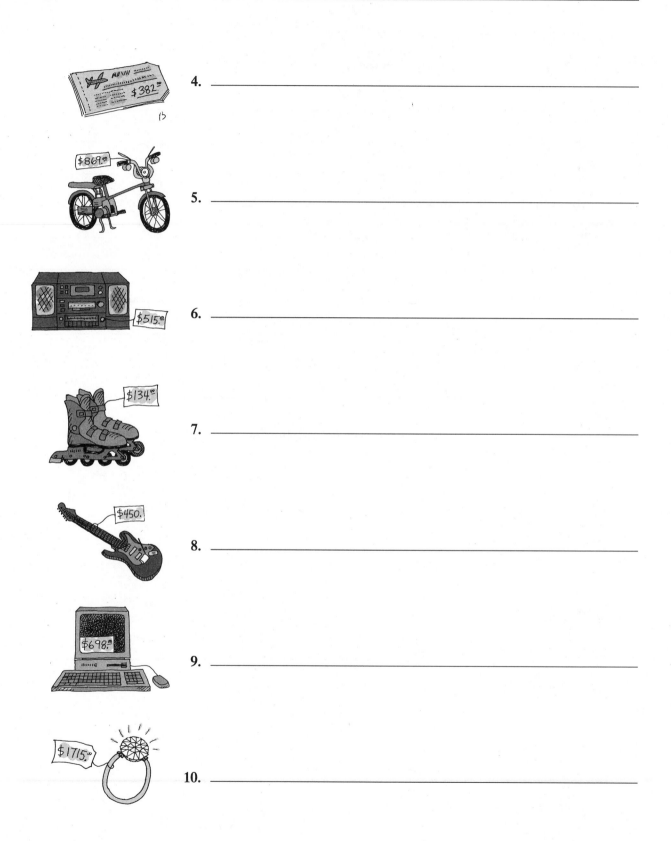

4. _____

5. _____

6. _____

7. _____

8. _____

9. _____

10. _____

J. **¿Cuántas personas hay en... ?** Write the number of people in words.

POPULATION OF SPANISH-SPEAKING COUNTRIES, 1995
Source: World Almanac and Book of Facts, 1996

Country	Population	Country	Population
Argentina	34,292,742	Mexico	93,985,848
Bolivia	7,896,254	Nicaragua	4,206,353
Chile	14,161,216	Panama	2,680,903
Colombia	36,200,251	Paraguay	5,358,198
Costa Rica	3,419,114	Peru	24,087,372
Cuba	10,937,635	Spain	39,404,348
Dominican Republic	7,948,223	Uruguay	3,222,716
Ecuador	10,890,950	Venezuela	21,004,773
El Salvador	5,870,481	*Puerto Rico	3,801,977
Guatemala	10,998,602	Puerto Ricans on mainland	2,700,000
Honduras	5,459,743	**United States (Hispanics)	26,800,000

*Estado Libre Asociado de Puerto Rico
**Total population 263,814,032

---

1. ¿Cuántas personas hay en España?

   _____

2. ¿Cuántas personas hay en México?

   _____

3. ¿Cuántas personas hay en (los) Estados Unidos?

   _____

4. ¿Cuántas personas hay en Guatemala?

   _____

5. ¿Cuántas personas hay en Honduras?

   _____

6. ¿Cuántas personas hay en El Salvador?

   _____

7. ¿Cuántas personas hay en Nicaragua?

   _____

8. ¿Cuántas personas hay en Costa Rica?

   _____

9. ¿Cuántas personas hay en Panamá?

_____

10. ¿Cuántas personas hay en Colombia?

_____

11. ¿Cuántas personas hay en Perú?

_____

12. ¿Cuántas personas hay en Chile?

_____

13. ¿Cuántas personas hay en Argentina?

_____

14. ¿Cuántas personas hay en Uruguay?

_____

15. ¿Cuántas personas hay en Paraguay?

_____

16. ¿Cuántas personas hay en Bolivia?

_____

17. ¿Cuántas personas hay en Venezuela?

_____

18. ¿Cuántas personas hay en Ecuador?

_____

19. ¿Cuántas personas hay en Cuba?

_____

20. ¿Cuántas personas hay en la República Dominicana?

_____

21. ¿Cuántas personas hay en Puerto Rico?

_____

Nombre_____

⋟ Unidad II Lección 1 ⋞

¿Cómo soy yo?
What do I look like?

VOCABULARIO   **La descripción física** *Physical description*

A. Write at least two adjectives in Spanish to describe each person in the drawings.

1. _____

2. _____

3. _____

4. _____

5. _____

6. _____

ESTRUCTURA   Yo *forms of* **ser**

B. Tell how you were, are, and will be. Write three sentences for each, using time expressions.

Yo no era alto de niño.

Yo soy más alto ahora.

En el futuro seré más alto.

1. _____

   _____

   _____

2. _____

   _____

   _____

3. _____

   _____

   _____

C. Think of a person you know or know about in each of the categories below and write in the information in each column.

CATEGORY OF PERSON	NAME	ADJECTIVES THAT DESCRIBE PERSON
historical figure	*Abraham Lincoln*	*alto, delgado, fuerte*
1. famous athlete	_____	_____
2. actor or actress	_____	_____
3. cartoon character	_____	_____
4. politician	_____	_____
5. a neighbor	_____	_____
6. your best friend	_____	_____

VOCABULARIO   Expresiones de tiempo *Time expressions*

D. Write in the Spanish expression that most accurately describes how often you do the activities listed, when you did them last, and when you will do them next time.

ACTIVITY	HOW OFTEN	LAST TIME	NEXT TIME
stay up all night	*raramente*	*hace dos meses*	*el próximo año*
1. walk to school			
2. cook a meal			
3. watch TV			
4. ride a bus			
5. travel to another state			
6. eat breakfast			
7. sleep well at night			
8. read the newspaper			

ESTRUCTURA   *Making a sentence negative*

E. Professor Vargas created a robot that repeats everything someone says. Today the robot is malfunctioning and is making every sentence negative. Can you predict how he will make these sentences negative? (Hint: Just put **no** in front of the verb.)

Ahora yo soy delgado. *Ahora yo no soy delgado.* _____

1. De niño yo era grande y fuerte. _____

2. A los sesenta años yo seré canoso. _____

3. El niño está aquí. _____

4. Tengo diez y seis años. _____

5. El avión es grande. _____

6. Llevo un suéter hoy. _____

7. Hay veinte estudiantes en la clase. _____

8. Yo como mucha fruta. _____

9. Son las diez de la mañana. _____

ESTRUCTURA *Comparing: so, more, or less*

F. It's your birthday and you're thinking about growing old. Do you think you will be more or less like the descriptions given below?

fuerte *En el futuro yo seré más fuerte.* _____

1. pequeño(a) _____

2. delgado(a) _____

3. débil _____

4. bajo(a) _____

5. guapo(a) _____

6. grande _____

7. alto(a) _____

8. feo(a) _____

9. bajo(a) _____

LEEMOS Y CONTAMOS

G. *Police lineup*   Here is an eyewitness description of three bank robbers given by a person who speaks only Spanish. Can you help the police identify the robbers from the pictures of some likely suspects? Put an *X* by the one you think is *not* a bank robber and then list a few of the physical characteristics you based your decision on.

DESCRIPCIÓN DE LOS LADRONES

Había tres ladrones: un hombre y dos mujeres. Él era guapo, mediano y moreno. Parecía ser muy fuerte. Una era débil, delgada, alta y bastante bonita. Ella tenía el pelo moreno. La otra era una morena fea, baja y muy gorda.

1. _____

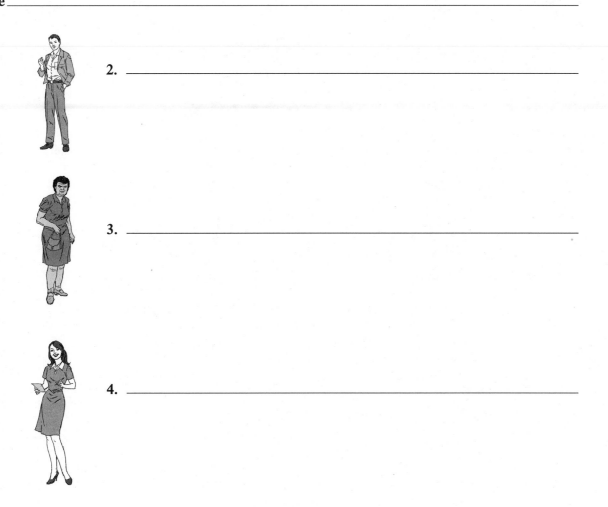

2. _____

3. _____

4. _____

H. Write the name and a description of the physical characteristics of a boy and a girl in your class. (Don't forget to make the adjectives feminine for the girl.)

1. El joven se llama _____ .

    Él es _____ .

2. La joven se llama _____ .

    Ella es _____ .

DIVERSIÓN

Buscapalabras How many of the adjectives of physical characteristics can you find in the square below? Write them in the blanks and then indicate whether you think they describe you or not. The words go forward, backward, and up and down diagonally.

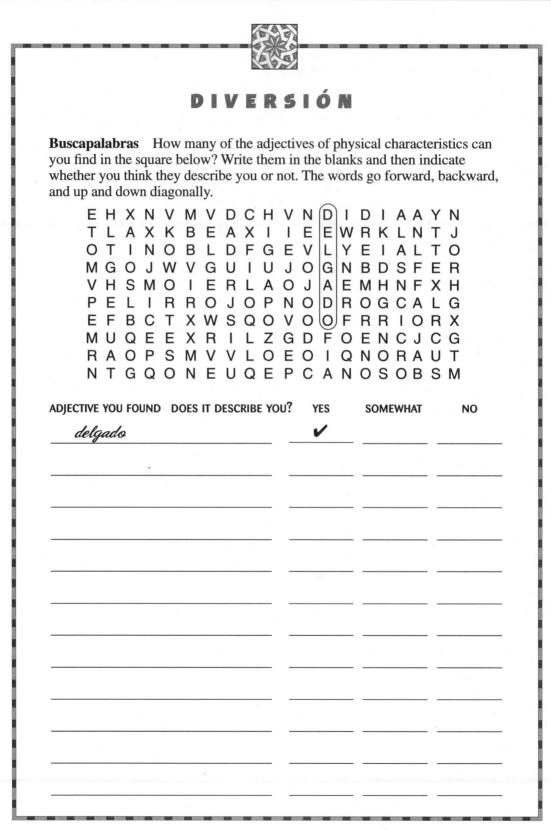

```
E H X N V M V D C H V N D I D I A A Y N
T L A X K B E A X I I E E W R K L N T J
O T I N O B L D F G E V L Y E I A L T O
M G O J W V G U I U J O G N B D S F E R
V H S M O I E R L A O J A E M H N F X H
P E L I R R O J O P N O D R O G C A L G
E F B C T X W S Q O V O O F R R I O R X
M U Q E E X R I L Z G D F O E N C J C G
R A O P S M V V L O E O I Q N O R A U T
N T G Q O N E U Q E P C A N O S O B S M
```

ADJECTIVE YOU FOUND	DOES IT DESCRIBE YOU?	YES	SOMEWHAT	NO
delgado		✔		

⇥ Unidad II Lección 2 ⇤

¿Cómo eres?
What are you like?

VOCABULARIO **La descripción de la personalidad** *Description of personality*

A. Write in an adjective of personality that you feel best describes the person in the drawing.

1. _____   2. _____

3. _____   4. _____

5. _____ 6. _____

7. _____ 8. _____

9. _____ 10. _____

B. Do you remember in Lesson 1 describing physical characteristics of people you know? Let's do the same thing now with personality characteristics. Write the information in each column.

CATEGORY OF PERSON	NAME	ADJECTIVES THAT DESCRIBE PERSON
historical figure	*Abraham Lincoln*	*inteligente, trabajador*
1. famous athlete		
2. actor or actress		
3. cartoon character		
4. politician		
5. a neighbor		
6. your best friend		
7. you!		

ESTRUCTURA *Forming yes/no questions*

C. Make each statement into a question three different ways:

    a. Leave it as it is and add question marks.

    b. Leave it as it is and add **¿no?** or **¿verdad?**

    c. Put the subject <u>after</u> the verb.

Tú eres trabajador.

    a. _*¿Tú eres trabajador?*_____

    b. _*Tú eres trabajador, ¿verdad?*_____

    c. _*¿Eres tú trabajador?*_____

1. Yo soy aburrido.

    a. _____

    b. _____

    c. _____

2. Paulina es estudiante.

    a. _____

    b. _____

    c. _____

3. Ricardo tiene quince años.

    a. _____

    b. _____

    c. _____

4. Los libros están en la mesa.

    a. _____

    b. _____

    c. _____

5. El Sr. Vargas es el profesor.

    a. _____

    b. _____

    c. _____

6. Ud. come chocolate.

    a. _____

    b. _____

    c. _____

7. La sopa es deliciosa.

a. _____

b. _____

c. _____

8. El teléfono está en la cocina.

a. _____

b. _____

c. _____

ESTRUCTURA *Making comparisons*

D. Compare yourself with people you know based on the qualities given.

fuerte *Roberto es más fuerte que yo.* _____

alto(a) *La profesora es tan alta como yo.* _____

1. simpático(a) _____

2. generoso(a) _____

3. popular _____

4. atlético(a) _____

5. ambicioso(a) _____

6. inteligente _____

7. feliz _____

8. aburrido(a) _____

9. egoísta _____

10. sincero(a) _____

LEEMOS Y CONTAMOS

E. You can play the matchmaker. Read each of the letters from the people below who are looking for someone to talk to. Draw a line between each pair you think is compatible. Explain what you found in the ads that made you think these people should talk to each other.

DSH-Dama simpática, de 27 años, muy educada, alegre, con deseos de gozar la vida; desea conocer caballero 30–35 años, educado, profesionista, de preferencia caribeño o con ascendencia italiana, que le guste bailar, la música alegre y los perritos pues yo tengo uno como mascota. EXT 3034

DSH-Muchacha hispana de 22 años, sincera, romántica, le gusta bailar, hacer ejercicios; desea conocer muchacho sincero, de 23–26 años que sea respetuoso y tenga buenos sentimientos. EXT 3458

DDH-Dama 25, años guapa y trabajadora, estudio enfermería; deseo conocer caballero, norteamericano de preferencia, de 25–40 años con deseos de establar una relación seria. EXT 3030

DSH-Joven de 24 años, super dinámica, alegre, deportista, profesionista, educada, no mal parecida, positiva, sin compromisos; desea conocer chico con las mismas cualidades, que le guste socializar, divertirse, estar al día con lo que pasa en el mundo y que opinar al respecto, no debe ser un super hombre pero sí un super caballero. EXT 3456

CSH-Caballero de 24 años, sudamericano, recién llegado de Florida, bien parecido, sin vicios, sin compromisos, muy divertido y educado; desea conocer chica simpática, alegre y educada que le guste divertirse sanamente y que me pueda enseñar Chicago. EXT 3031

CSH-Atractivo joven de 29 años, ojiverde, cuerpo atlético, mexicano desea conocer chica de 20–25 años, simpática, comprensiva, con buena personalidad, para disfrutar juntos de los deportes, conciertos, paseos al parque o a la playa y un sinfín de diversiones sanas. EXT 3426

CSH-Soy un caballero de 35 años, sencillo, respetuoso, sin compromisos y busco una compañera de 25–38 años, sincera, cariñosa y comprensiva que también este buscando un compañero para pasar sus ratos libres y compartir diversiones sanas, pláticas, etc. EXT 3435

CSH-Caballero mexicano, trabajador, sincero, alegre; desea conocer dama hispana, de 18–25 años, sin compromisos, hogareña, sincera no importa la apariencia física. EXT 3423

Pair #1. I.D. numbers _____ and _____

Why are they compatible? _____

Pair #2. I.D. numbers _____ and _____

Why are they compatible? _____

Pair #3. I.D. numbers _____ and _____

Why are they compatible? _____

F. Now it's your turn to send in a "Lonely Hearts" ad. Here are some questions someone might ask you. Write as much as you can to answer the questions. Some sample answers are given, but make up your own. You may want to review the vocabulary and function phrases in the Tools section for Unit I in your textbook.

¿Cómo eres tú? _Yo soy baja y morena. No soy muy bonita, pero soy inteligente y muy simpática._

1. ¿Qué te gusta? _Me gusta eschuchar música, bailar y cantar. Me gustan las personas sinceras y honestas. No me gustan los perros._

2. ¿Qué tienes tú? _Yo tengo muchos amigos y una familia grande. Tengo una bicicleta y una computadora en casa._

G. Now fill out the form on the newspaper page and then write a short description of yourself and the kind of person you would like to meet.

Llene los siguientes datos.
Recorte y envie este cupón a:

AMOR PARA TODOS
3909 N. Cleveland Chicago IL 60613
O Llame al (312) 525-6325. Pregunte por Rosa

CLAVES PARA SU AVISO

D: dama	B: blanca/o
C: caballero	S: soltera/o
H: hispana/o	D: divorciada/o
N: negra/o	V: viuda/o

Nombre: _____

Dirección: _____ ZIP: _____

Teléfono: _____

Descripción física: _____

Aficiones: _____

Edad: _____

Edad de la persona que busca: _____

Sexo de la persona que busca: _____

Descripción de la persona que busca: _____
_____

DIVERSIÓN

Crucigrama *Crossword puzzle* Use the clues to fill in the appropriate Spanish adjectives of personality characteristics. (Refer to the vocabulary list on page 141 in your textbook.)

Einstein, the famous scientist was ___*inteligente*_____ .

1. A person who gives a lot of money to charity is _____ .

2. Someone who wants to get ahead in life is _____ .

3. When your favorite pet dies you are very _____ .

4. Anyone who participates in the Olympic Games must be very _____ .

5. The opposite of hardworking is _____ .

6. If you won the lottery you would be very _____ .

7. Someone who is afraid to talk to people is _____ .

8. If you talk only about yourself, you are _____ .

9. A person who has a lot of friends is _____ .

Now use the answers for 1 to 10 above to fill in the following word grid. The first one is already done for you. Count the number of spaces in the grid to select the appropriate word. Be sure that crossing words share the same letter where they intersect.

Nombre _____

⟶ Unidad II Lección 3 ⟵

¿De dónde es usted, señor?
Where are you from, sir?

ESTRUCTURA   Usted *forms of* ser

A. Everyone hopes to be better in the future. Here are ten statements of what these people used to be like. Encourage them by telling something positive about them in the future. Use the **Ud.** form of **ser.** (Review adjectives in Lessons 1 and 2 for opposites.)

Yo era perezoso. _*En el futuro Ud. será trabajador.*_____

1. Yo era gordo. _____

2. Yo era callado. _____

3. Yo era bajo. _____

4. Yo era tonta. _____

5. Yo era tímido. _____

6. Yo era fea. _____

7. Yo era débil. _____

8. Yo era aburrida. _____

9. Yo era antipático. _____

10. Yo era triste. _____

CONVERSACIÓN *Asking and telling national origins*

B. Tell what country a person is from if he or she is a certain nationality. Use the **Ud.** form of **ser.**

Si Ud. es francés, *Ud. es de Francia.* _____

1. Si Ud. es inglesa, _____.

2. Si Ud. es alemán, _____.

3. Si Ud. es norteamericano, _____.

4. Si Ud. es español, _____.

5. Si Ud. es costarricense, _____.

6. Si Ud. es escocés, _____.

7. Si Ud. es italiana, _____.

8. Si Ud. es ruso, _____.

9. Si Ud. es griego, _____.

C. Now tell what a person's nationality is if he or she is from a certain country.

Si Ud. es de Japón, *Ud. es japonés.* _____

1. Si Ud. es de Portugal, _____.

2. Si Ud. es de Canadá, _____.

3. Si Ud. es de Panamá, _____.

4. Si Ud. es de Cuba, _____.

5. Si Ud. es de África, _____.

6. Si Ud. es de Brasil, _____.

7. Si Ud. es de Ecuador, _____.

8. Si Ud. es de Perú, _____.

9. Si Ud. es de Paraguay, _____.

Nombre _____

D. Inés is doing a story for the school newspaper. Here are her notes from an interview. What questions did she ask? Write in an appropriate question for each answer. Use the formal **Ud.**

¿Quién es Ud.? ¿Cómo se llama Ud.? _____ Yo soy Ramón Salinas.

1. _____ Estoy bien, gracias.

2. _____ Yo soy de Panamá.

3. _____ Soy bajo y moreno.

4. _____ Estoy aquí porque es interesante.

5. _____ Yo tengo veinte y seis años.

6. _____ Mi cumpleaños es el dos de junio.

7. _____ Mi padre es Roberto Salinas.

LEEMOS Y CONTAMOS

E. Read Mr. Vargas's horoscope. Then tell in English what his future will be like.

> En el pasado Ud. era pobre y sin mucho dinero. Pero hoy Ud. es un hombre muy afortunado. Ud. será muy famoso algún día. Ud. tendrá mucho dinero y será muy rico. También será padre de una familia grande con cinco hijos y diez nietos. Su casa será muy grande con ocho alcobas, cuatro baños y una ancha escalera circular.

What will Mr. Vargas's future be?

_____

_____

_____

_____

_____

F. Now write a prediction in Spanish for your teacher (just for fun)! Don't forget to be courteous and use the **Ud.** form of **ser.**

Querido(a) profesor(a),

_____

_____

_____

D I V E R S I Ó N

Palabras cifradas   The first column is a list of Spanish-speaking countries. Unscramble the nationalities in the third column. Then write the nationality and the number of the country in the second column.

COUNTRY	NATIONALITY	SCRAMBLED NATIONALITY
1. Bolivia	*colombiano 3*	bcomlonioa
2. El Salvador		niviloabo
3. Colombia		cniomdiona
4. Argentina		yuruaoug
5. Chile		idasetuonsened
6. Venezuela		icnxemoa
7. Guatemala		gacirnaesneü
8. México		erdonuhoñ
9. Estados Unidos		onelovenaz
10. Nicaragua		vdoñaseoarl
11. Uruguay		nhclieo
12. Honduras		ganertain
13. la República Dominicana		talemaceoug

⇛ Unidad II Lección 4 ⇜
Mi familia
My family

VOCABULARIO   **Los miembros de la familia** *Family members*

A. Describe the relationship of each person in the family tree to the others in the family as indicated.

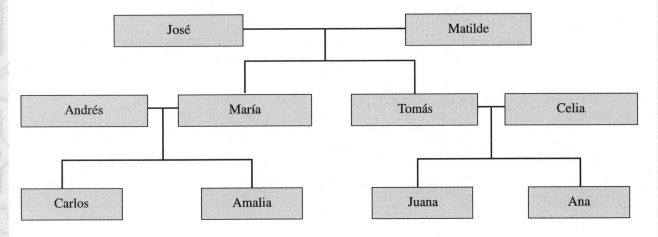

1. José

es el _____*esposo*_____ de Matilde.

es el _____ de María.

es el _____ de Carlos.

es el _____ de Andrés.

2. Matilde

es la _____ de José.

es la _____ de María.

es la _____ de Carlos.

es la _____ de Andrés.

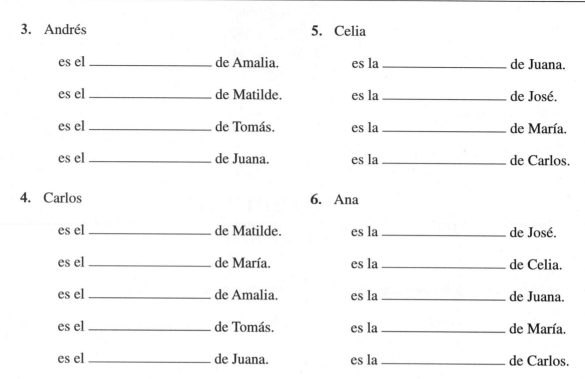

3. Andrés

    es el _____ de Amalia.

    es el _____ de Matilde.

    es el _____ de Tomás.

    es el _____ de Juana.

4. Carlos

    es el _____ de Matilde.

    es el _____ de María.

    es el _____ de Amalia.

    es el _____ de Tomás.

    es el _____ de Juana.

5. Celia

    es la _____ de Juana.

    es la _____ de José.

    es la _____ de María.

    es la _____ de Carlos.

6. Ana

    es la _____ de José.

    es la _____ de Celia.

    es la _____ de Juana.

    es la _____ de María.

    es la _____ de Carlos.

ESTRUCTURA *Identifying and describing other people*

B. Identify three people in your family. Tell what their relationship is to you. Then describe each in the <u>past</u> **(era),** <u>present</u> **(es),** and <u>future</u> **(será).**

PERSON	*Stephen es mi primo.*
PAST	*En el pasado él era débil.*
PRESENT	*Ahora él es fuerte.*
FUTURE	*En el futuro él será importante.*

1. PERSON _____

    PAST _____

    PRESENT _____

    FUTURE _____

  2. PERSON   _____

     PAST   _____

     PRESENT   _____

     FUTURE   _____

  3. PERSON   _____

     PAST   _____

     PRESENT   _____

     FUTURE   _____

ESTRUCTURA   *Telling where someone is from*

C. There is a national convention of Latino business executives in town. Everyone is wearing a name badge with his or her name and city. Tell where each person is from.

José Zamora/San Diego, CA   *José Zamora es de San Diego.*

  1. Carolina Quijano/Omaha, NE _____

_____

  2. Esteban Hijosa/Santa Fe, NM _____

_____

  3. Felicia Villalobos/Chicago, IL _____

_____

  4. Marcos Sarmiento/New Haven, CT _____

_____

  5. Rosa Domínguez/Atlanta, GA _____

_____

ESTRUCTURA   *Gender of nouns*

D.   Write **el** for masculine words and **la** for feminine words.

1. _____ escritor   6. _____ ciudad   11. _____ nación

2. _____ pañuelo   7. _____ vela   12. _____ albañil

3. _____ mano   8. _____ mentalidad 13. _____ día

4. _____ tocador   9. _____ sección   14. _____ sinfonía

5. _____ tamal   10. _____ coro   15. _____ senador

ESTRUCTURA   *Showing ownership*

E.   Describe the relationship of five members of your family to another member.

_____*Mi tío Michael es el hermano de mi madre.*_____

1. _____

2. _____

3. _____

4. _____

5. _____

F.   Write a sentence next to each drawing to explain who these things belong to. Remember, you cannot use an apostrophe + *s* to show possession in Spanish. You may want to review names of things on pages 8-9 in your textbook.

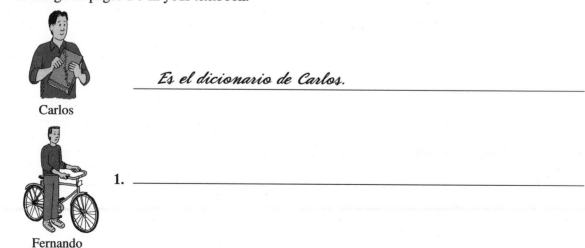

Carlos

_____*Es el dicionario de Carlos.*_____

Fernando

1. _____

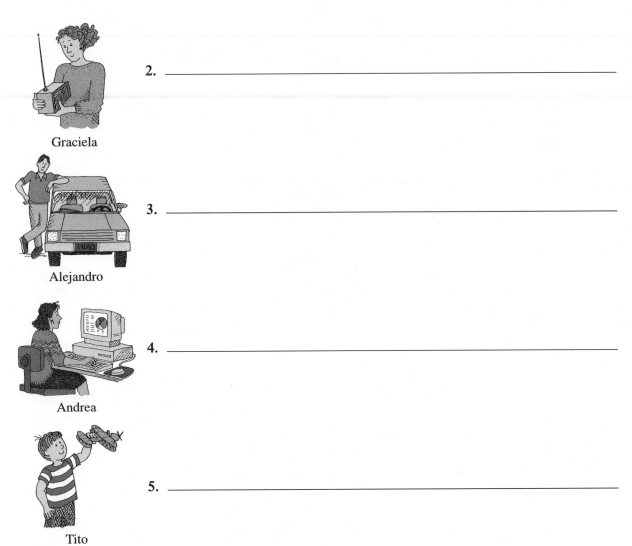

Graciela

2. _____

Alejandro

3. _____

Andrea

4. _____

Tito

5. _____

ESTRUCTURA *Defining* **su**

G. Now explain who the objects in Activity F belong to by saying *It's his or her . . .* Then clarify **su** by using **de él** or **de ella.**

Es su diccionario. Es el diccionario de él.

1. _____

2. _____

3. _____

4. _____

5. _____

LEEMOS Y CONTAMOS

H. Juana is describing the pictures in a family photo album to her friends. Read what she says.

Aquí está mi primo Carlos. Él tiene una motocicleta muy rápida. Y aquí está mi hermana gemela, Ana, con su perro grande. En esta foto está mi padre con su cartera nueva y mi madre con sus gafas rojas. Aquí mi tío lleva un traje pardo oscuro y mi tía lleva un vestido morado. Y aquí en esta foto está mi abuelo con una nueva computadora.

Juana wants to be sure that you understood. Tell her who owns these things.

a fast motorcycle   *tu primo Carlos*

1. a big dog

2. a new briefcase

3. red glasses

4. a dark brown suit

5. a purple dress

6. a new computer

I. Now it's your turn to describe some things five members of your family have. Refer to the list of things in the Tools for Unit I for ideas.

Mi primo tiene un sombrero negro.

1.

2.

3.

4.

5.

⇢ Unidad II Lección 5 ⇠

¿Qué serás en el futuro?
What will you be in the future?

VOCABULARIO   **Las profesiones** *Occupations*

A. Write the name of the profession of each of the following.

la ingeniera _____

1. _____

2. _____

3. _____

4. _____

5. _____

6. _____

7. _____

8. _____

9. _____

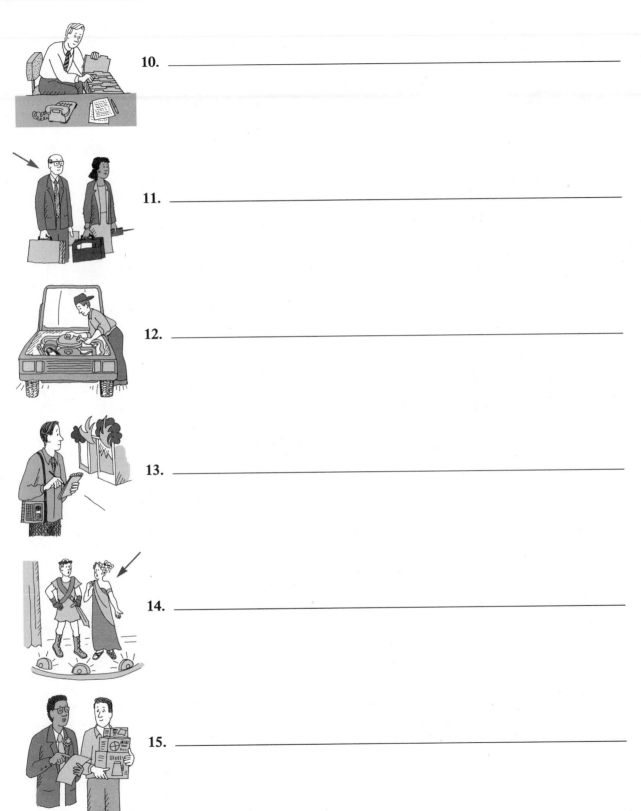

10. _____

11. _____

12. _____

13. _____

14. _____

15. _____

16. _____

17. _____

18. _____

19. _____

20. _____

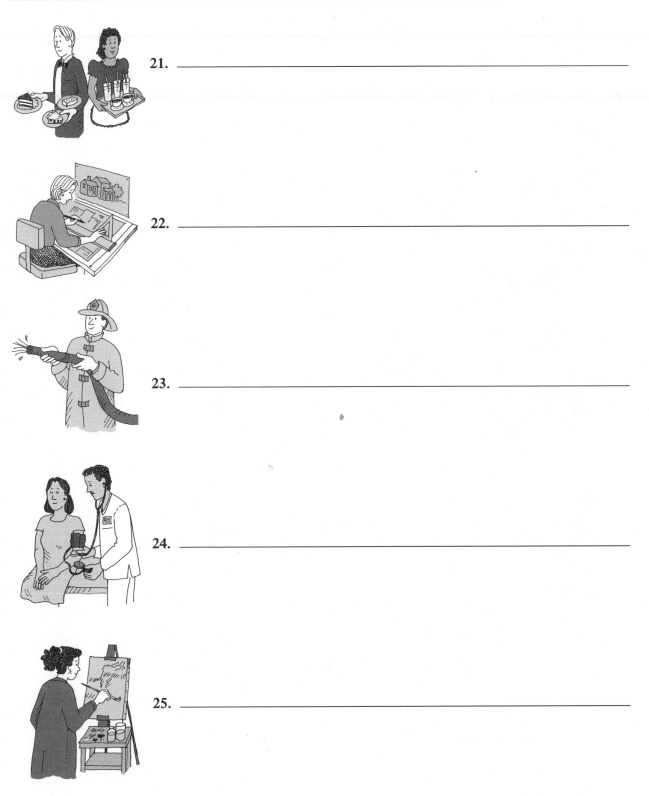

21. _____

22. _____

23. _____

24. _____

25. _____

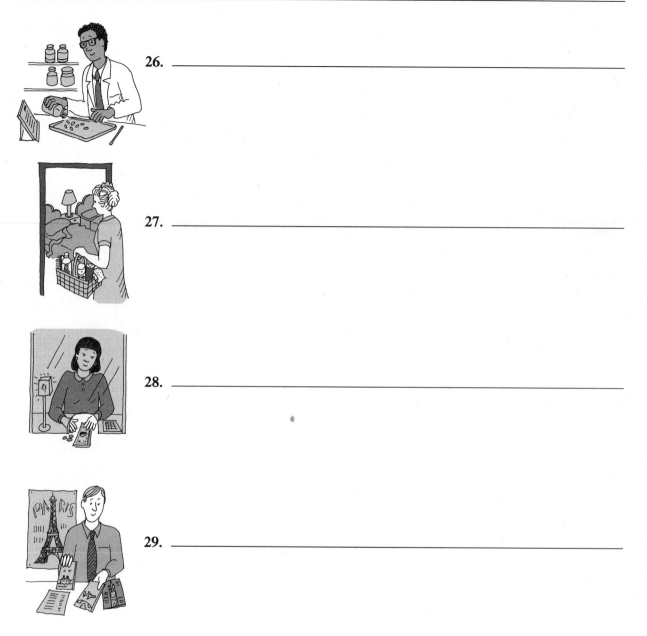

26. _____

27. _____

28. _____

29. _____

ESTRUCTURA *Making nouns and adjectives plural, Plural forms* los *and* las

B. Write the plural of each of the following articles and nouns.

el libro _____*los libros*_____

1. el papel _____

2. la mesa _____

3. el reloj _____

4. la nación _____

5. el actor _____

6. la actriz _____

7. el hombre _____

8. el día _____

9. la mujer _____

10. el lápiz _____

ESTRUCTURA *Plural adjectives with plural nouns*

C. Describe what characteristics you think people in these professions often have. There are many possible answers for each. See the Tools for Unit II for ideas.

profesor _____*Los profesores son inteligentes.*_____

1. bombero _____

2. actriz _____

3. enfermera _____

4. banquero _____

5. agricultor _____

ESTRUCTURA   Nosotros *form of* ser

D. Describe a characteristic you have in common with five different friends.

_____*Mi amiga Josefina y yo somos generosos.*_____

1. _____

2. _____

3. _____

4. _____

5. _____

6. _____

7. _____

8. _____

ESTRUCTURA   Ustedes (Uds.) *form of* ser

E. Tell the following people what you think they were like in the past and what you think they will be like in the future.

   tus padres

_____*En el pasado Uds. eran pobres.*_____

_____*En el futuro Uds. serán ricos.*_____

1. tus amigos

_____

_____

2. tus profesores

_____

_____

3. tus compañeros de clase *(classmates)*

_____

_____

4. tus… *(your choice)*

_____

_____

LEEMOS Y CONTAMOS

F. Read these employment ads. Make a list in English of the characteristics and qualifications the employer wants.

EMPRESA LÍDER
Solicita:

OBREROS GENERALES

Requisitos:
- Edad de 20 a 35 años.
- Conocimientos básicos de mecánica.
- Sin problemas de horario.

Ofrecemos:
- Atractivo sueldo.
- Fondo de ahorro, Ayuda de transporte, Bonos de despensa, Premio de puntualidad, Reembolso de notas, Seguro de vida, Comedor, Entre otros.

Interesados presentarse en:
Modeso Arrola 604-01

AMUROL, MÉXICO, S.A. DE C. V. SOLICITA

SECRETARIA
AYUDANTE DE CONTABILIDAD

Requisitos:
- Soltera
- Experiencia mínima un año

CHOFER

- Con experiencia

Interesados presentarse con
curriculum vitae en
Blvd. Díaz Ordaz 131, Sta. Catarina, M.L.
De 9:00 A.M. a 3:00 P.M.

---

1. _____

_____

_____

_____

2. _____

_____

_____

_____

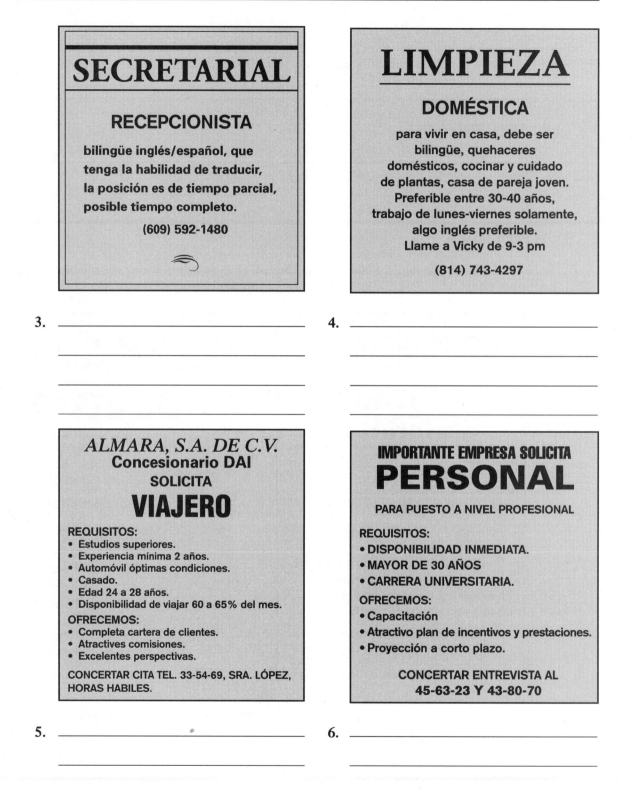

SECRETARIAL

RECEPCIONISTA

bilingüe inglés/español, que
tenga la habilidad de traducir,
la posición es de tiempo parcial,
posible tiempo completo.

(609) 592-1480

LIMPIEZA

DOMÉSTICA

para vivir en casa, debe ser
bilingüe, quehaceres
domésticos, cocinar y cuidado
de plantas, casa de pareja joven.
Preferible entre 30-40 años,
trabajo de lunes-viernes solamente,
algo inglés preferible.
Llame a Vicky de 9-3 pm

(814) 743-4297

3. _____

4. _____

ALMARA, S.A. DE C.V.
Concesionario DAI
SOLICITA
VIAJERO

REQUISITOS:
- Estudios superiores.
- Experiencia mínima 2 años.
- Automóvil óptimas condiciones.
- Casado.
- Edad 24 a 28 años.
- Disponibilidad de viajar 60 a 65% del mes.

OFRECEMOS:
- Completa cartera de clientes.
- Atractives comisiones.
- Excelentes perspectivas.

**CONCERTAR CITA TEL. 33-54-69, SRA. LÓPEZ,
HORAS HABILES.**

IMPORTANTE EMPRESA SOLICITA
PERSONAL
PARA PUESTO A NIVEL PROFESIONAL

REQUISITOS:
- DISPONIBILIDAD INMEDIATA.
- MAYOR DE 30 AÑOS
- CARRERA UNIVERSITARIA.

OFRECEMOS:
- Capacitación
- Atractivo plan de incentivos y prestaciones.
- Proyección a corto plazo.

**CONCERTAR ENTREVISTA AL
45-63-23 Y 43-80-70**

5. _____

6. _____

G. Compose your own ad. Choose an occupation and write some characteristics you want in the person you are looking for.

Se busca criada.
Debe ser honesta, trabajadora, inteligente,
sincera, fuerte para limpiar una casa
con tres alcobas y dos baños. Se paga $6.00 per hora.
Llame al teléfono 234-9902 por la tarde.

DIVERSIÓN

Adivinanzas From the Spanish list in this lesson, choose a profession that fits the description in each clue and write the number in the blank.

1. I work on people's teeth.   _____ mecánico

2. I sing and dance.   _____ periodista

3. I have a green thumb.   _____ bombero

4. I fill prescriptions.   _____ profesor

5. I play a piano.   _____ secretario

6. I study a lot.   _____ ingeniero

7. I clean houses.   _____ contador

8. I build bridges.   ___1___ dentista

9. I take care of sick people.   _____ actriz

10. I work in a school.   _____ banquero

11. I handle a lot of money.   _____ farmacista

12. I fight fires.   _____ estudiante

13. I'm good with numbers.   _____ agricultor

14. I fix cars.   _____ criado

15. I can type very fast.   _____ músico

16. I write for a newspaper.   _____ enfermero

Nombre_____

⇒ Unidad II Lección 6 ⇐

En el aula
In the classroom

VOCABULARIO   **Las cosas en el aula** *Classroom objects*

A. Identify each of the following classroom objects.

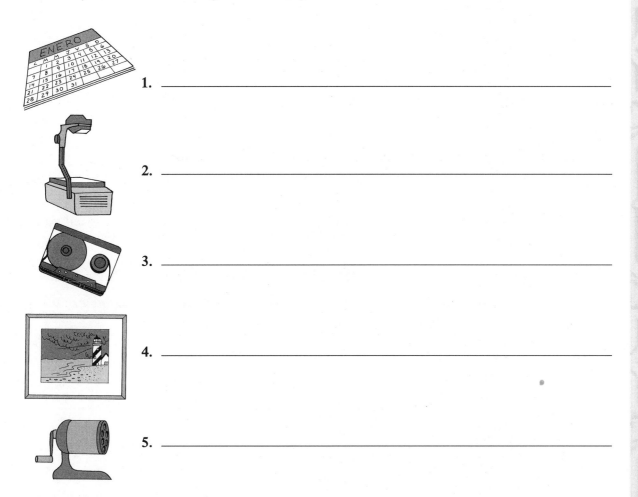

1. _____

2. _____

3. _____

4. _____

5. _____

6. _____

7. _____

8. _____

9. _____

VOCABULARIO   Los colores, las formas y los tamaños *Colors, shapes, and sizes*

ESTRUCTURA   *Existence, Indefinite articles, singular and plural*

B. Tell if there are the following items in your classroom and, if so, how many. Also tell if the same objects were in your last class and if you think they will be in your next class.

escritorio grande   *Hay un escritorio grande en esta clase. Había un escritorio*

grande en mi clase anterior y no habrá un escritorio grande en mi

próxima clase.

1. bandera española _____

_____

_____

2. pizarra verde _____

_____

_____

3. pupitres nuevos _____

_____

_____

4. papeleras redondas _____

_____

_____

5. estudiantes inteligentes _____

_____

_____

ESTRUCTURA Ser *forms with things, Descriptive adjectives*

C. Rewrite the following sentences, making the noun plural. Make all other necessary changes. Pay careful attention to the tense of the verb.

El libro es azul. _____*Los libros son azules.*_____

1. La grabadora es vieja. _____

2. La pizarra será larga. _____

3. El globo será redondo. _____

4. La mochila era marrón. _____

5. El diccionario era pesado. _____

6. El aula es pequeña. _____

ESTRUCTURA   *Comparing objects*

D. Compare some of your family's things with those of a neighbor or relative.

Nuestra casa es tan grande como su casa.

1. _____

2. _____

3. _____

4. _____

5. _____

6. _____

7. _____

8. _____

ESTRUCTURA   *The most . . . The least . . . (Superlatives)*

E. Here is a list of items that many people have. Tell who in your class has the *most* and *least [adj.]*.

una cartera nueva   *El profesor tiene la cartera más nueva de la clase.*

1. un lápiz corto _____

2. una goma pequeña _____

3. una calculadora cara _____

4. un cuaderno pesado _____

5. un libro grande _____

6. una mochila ligera _____

7. un diccionario barato _____

LEEMOS Y CONTAMOS

F. Read about schools of the past and present and answer the question that follows.

En el pasado en los Estados Unidos había escuelas con una sola sala de clase que no tenían tantas cosas como hay en las escuelas de hoy. En estas escuelas no había electricidad y a veces los estudiantes no tenían libros, ni cuadernos ni lápices. No había radios, teléfonos, discos, autobuses ni grabadoras de vídeo. Y claro, no había computadoras. Frecuentemente no había pupitres; a veces había sólo sillas y mesas viejas. Ahora hay todo lo necesario en las escuelas de los Estados Unidos, pero en muchos de los países de Latinoamérica hay una situación casi tan mala como en las escuelas norteamericanas del pasado.

Can you list at least ten things (in English) that schools of the past may not have had that we take for granted now? Where do schools like this still exist?

*electricity*_____

1. _____   6. _____

2. _____   7. _____

3. _____   8. _____

4. _____   9. _____

5. _____   10. _____

G. Describe what you think classrooms will be like in the future. Write at least five sentences.

Habrá más computadoras grandes y un sacapuntas eléctrico. No habrá

tantos libros como ahora.

_____

_____

_____

_____

_____

_____

DIVERSIÓN

Match the description with the classroom object. Write the letter of the object in the space provided. Then fill in the crossword with the appropriate Spanish word.

1. _____ I make a point of sharpening things.   **a.** la goma

2. _____ I'm very patriotic and colorful.   **b.** el mapa

3. _____ I'm very good at remembering dates.   **c.** el diccionario

4. _____ I keep time with my hands.   **d.** la grabadora

5. _____ I can write very well, but I need your help.   **e.** las tijeras

6. _____ In your classroom I'm bilingual, but in English class I'm not. **f.** el calendario

7. _____ Your finger can travel on me to distant lands.   **g.** el reloj

8. _____ If you make a mistake, I can take care of it.   **h.** el sacapuntas

9. _____ I can talk, but only if you tell me what to say.   **i.** el lápiz

10. _____ I'll cut you if you're not careful.   **j.** la bandera

❧ Unidad II Structure Review ❧

PAULINA, SU FAMILIA Y SUS AMIGOS

Note: Review Tools section in the textbook at the beginning of Unit II before doing the activities in this Unit summary.

Subject Pronouns (Lesson 1)

A. **¿Quién?** Which Spanish pronoun would Paulina use in each of the following situations?

_____*yo*_____ She talks about herself.

1. _____ She talks about her family and herself.

2. _____ She talks to her friend Rosita.

3. _____ She talks to her mother.

4. _____ She talks to both her parents. (She is *not* from Spain.)

5. _____ If she were from Spain, how would she address her parents?

6. _____ She talks to her teacher.

7. _____ She talks about her cousin Eduardo.

8. _____ She talks about her parents.

9. _____ She talks about her friend Rosita.

10. _____ She talks about her friends Rosita and Adela.

11. _____ She talks about her friends Rosita, Jaime, and Salvador.

The verb ser (to be) (Lesson 5)

B. Paulina y su familia   Complete the paragraph with the correct forms of the verb **ser** in the <u>present</u> tense.

Hola, yo ____*soy*____ Paulina Rodríguez. Mi familia _____ americana
1

pero mis abuelos _____ de México. Mi padre _____ abogado y
2 3

mi madre _____ ingeniera. Mis hermanos _____ mayores que
4 5

yo y mi hermana _____ menor. Roberto _____ mecánico y
6 7

Tomás _____ enfermero. Yo _____ estudiante y Carlota
8 9

_____ estudiante también. Y tú, ¿ _____ estudiante también?
10 11

¿Tu familia y tú _____ americanos? Tengo muchos amigos. Rosita
12

_____ mi mejor amiga. Ella y yo _____ estudiantes en la
13 14

misma (same) clase.

C. Jaime es mi novio.   Complete the paragraph with the correct forms of the verb **ser** in the <u>present</u> tense.

Jaime ____*es*____ mi mejor amigo. También _____ mi novio.
1

_____ alto, guapo y muy simpático. Sus padres _____ de México
2 3

pero Jaime y su hermana _____ americanos. Yo _____ feliz
4 5

porque Jaime y yo _____ amigos. ¿ _____ Uds. amigos de
6 7

él también? ¿No? ¡Qué lástima!

D. Diego y Jorge eran los novios de Paulina.   Complete the paragraph with the correct forms of the verb **ser** in the <u>past</u> (imperfect) tense.

Diego y Jorge ____*eran*____ mis novios. Diego _____ mi novio cuando
1

yo tenía trece años (I was thirteen) y Jorge _____ mi novio cuando yo tenía trece
2

años y medio. Los dos _____ altos y guapos y también _____ muy
3 4

simpáticos. Jorge _____ más listo que Diego. Nosotros _____
5 6

amigos antes de ser novios. Yo _____ muy joven cuando yo
7

_____ su novia. ¿Quién _____ tu novio(a) a los trece años?
8 9

E. **El año que viene** *Next year* Complete the paragraph with the correct forms of the verb **ser** in the <u>future</u> tense.

El año que viene Jaime y yo ___*seremos*___ estudiantes en la escuela secundaria y

también _____ novios. Nuestros mejores amigos _____ Rosita
          1   2

y Raúl. Yo _____ una buena estudiante y Jaime _____ un buen
          3   4

estudiante también porque nos gusta la escuela. Nosotros _____ muy serios y
                                             5

también nosotros _____ muy listos. La escuela _____ muy
                  6   7

divertida *(fun)* pero las clases _____ difíciles y los profesores
                                  8

_____ muy estrictos. Yo _____ muy ambiciosa y
         9   10

_____ la mejor estudiante de mi clase. Y tú, ¿cómo _____
        11   12

el año que viene? ¿ _____ tú buen estudiante también?
                   13

¿Quién _____ tu novio(a)?
         14

Negative sentences (Lesson 1)

F. **Paulina y Jaime no son novios.** Jaime and Paulina just had an argument about his not calling or visiting her over the weekend. Paulina is afraid that they may be breaking up and she is upset. Her friend Rosita is trying to make her feel better. Whenever Paulina says something good about Jaime, Rosita tells her the opposite.

    Paulina: Jaime es muy guapo.

    Rosita: ___*Jaime no es guapo.*_____

1. Jaime es muy sincero. _____

2. Es muy simpático. _____

3. Es muy listo. _____

4. Es muy generoso. _____

5. Es muy interesante. _____

G. **Paulina, tú no tienes la culpa.** *Paulina, it's not your fault.* Paulina blames herself for the argument. Rosita tells her that's not so.

    Paulina: Soy muy aburrida.

    Rosita: _____¡No, tú no eres aburrida!_____

1. Soy muy egoísta. _____

2. Soy muy perezosa. _____

3. Soy muy tímida. _____

4. Soy muy fea. _____

5. Soy muy tonta. _____

Yes/no questions (Lesson 2)

H. **Paulina y Jaime son novios otra vez.** Jaime apologized to Paulina for not calling her and now they are **novios** again. Paulina is telling Rosita how she feels about Jaime.

    sincero   Rosita: _____¿Es sincero Jaime?_____

                  Paulina: _____Sí, es muy sincero._____

1. simpático   Rosita: _____

                   Paulina: _____

2. amable   Rosita: _____

                   Paulina: _____

3. generoso   Rosita: _____

                   Paulina: _____

4. interesante   Rosita: _____

                   Paulina: _____

   5. popular   Rosita: _____

                    Paulina: _____

   6. guapo   Rosita: _____

                    Paulina: _____

   7. atlético   Rosita: _____

                    Paulina: _____

I. ¿Siempre será... ? Rosita wants to know if Paulina thinks Jaime will still be the same in the future. Paulina assures her that he will be.

   sincero   Rosita: *Jaime siempre será sincero, ¿verdad? (¿no?)*

                    Paulina: *Sí, siempre será sincero.*

   1. simpático   Rosita: _____

                    Paulina: _____

   2. amable   Rosita: _____

                    Paulina: _____

   3. generoso   Rosita: _____

                    Paulina: _____

   4. interesante   Rosita: _____

                    Paulina: _____

   5. popular   Rosita: _____

                    Paulina: _____

   6. guapo   Rosita: _____

                    Paulina: _____

   7. atlético   Rosita: _____

                    Paulina: _____

J. **¿Era guapo Jorge?** Rosita wants to know if Paulina's old boyfriend Jorge had the same qualities as Jaime. Paulina is certain that he didn't and that he never **(nunca)** will compare to Jaime. Write Rosita's questions and Paulina's answer to show this.

popular Rosita: _¿Era guapo Jorge?_

Paulina: _No, él no era tan guapo y nunca será tan_

guapo como Jaime.

1. amable Rosita: _____

Paulina: _____

_____

2. simpático Rosita: _____

Paulina: _____

_____

3. sincero Rosita: _____

Paulina: _____

_____

4. ambicioso Rosita: _____

Paulina: _____

_____

5. generoso Rosita: _____

Paulina: _____

_____

Information questions (Lesson 3)

K. **¿Quién es Eduardo?** Paulina's cousin Eduardo has just arrived from México for a visit. Rosita telephones to find out about him. Eduardo hears Paulina's answers. Can you help him guess what Rosita's questions were?

Es mi primo.

¿Quién es? _____

1. Se llama Eduardo.

_____

2. Es alto, moreno y un poco tímido.

_____

3. Es estudiante ahora, pero será periodista.

_____

4. Es de México.

_____

5. Está muy bien.

_____

6. Hay tres hermanos en la familia.

_____

L. **¿Quién era la chica?** As luck would have it, Eduardo saw Rosita when she came to pick up Paulina for school. He would like to know something about her. What are some questions he might ask Paulina when she returns?

¿Quién era la chica? _____

_____

_____

_____

_____

_____

_____

_____

_____

_____

_____

_____

Gender of nouns (Lesson 4)

M. **El señor González** The Spanish teacher, Señor González, dropped the word cards and they scattered. Paulina volunteered to sort the cards for him. She has to put them into two piles, one for masculine nouns, the other for feminine nouns. Make a list of the masculine nouns and the feminine nouns for her.

MASCULINE NOUNS	FEMININE NOUNS
el diccionario	*la bandera*

Plural of nouns (Lesson 5)

N. **Un perro, dos perros** Using Señor González's "word cards" from Activity M, practice making nouns plural.

diccionario

bandera

país

gemelo

mujer

dependienta

hermana

reloj

papel

hombre

papelera

nieta

libro

madre

ciudad

instrucción

archivador

globo

descripción

profesor

nacionalidad

amiga

lápiz

pupitre

MASCULINE PLURAL	FEMININE PLURAL
los diccionarios	*las banderas*

Articles (Lessons 4, 6)

O. **Me gustan los suéteres azules** Paulina and Rosita go shopping. Paulina wants to buy some things that are similar to those she already has. Write the conversation between the two girls. Follow the example.

un suéter azul

Rosita: _____ *Tú ya* (already) *tienes un suéter azul.* _____

Paulina: _____ *Sí, pero me gustan los suéteres azules.* _____

1. un libro romántico

Rosita: _____

Paulina: _____

2. una camisa roja

Rosita: _____

Paulina: _____

3. un disco popular

Rosita: _____

Paulina: _____

4. una falda corta

Rosita: _____

Paulina: _____

5. un vestido largo

Rosita: _____

Paulina: _____

6. una blusa bonita

Rosita: _____

Paulina: _____

P. La clase del señor González Complete the following paragraph about Señor González's class. The definite article **(el/la/los/las)** has been left out.

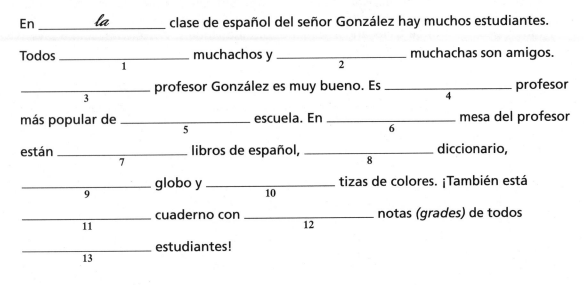

En _____ *la* _____ clase de español del señor González hay muchos estudiantes.

Todos _____ 1 _____ muchachos y _____ 2 _____ muchachas son amigos.

_____ 3 _____ profesor González es muy bueno. Es _____ 4 _____ profesor

más popular de _____ 5 _____ escuela. En _____ 6 _____ mesa del profesor

están _____ 7 _____ libros de español, _____ 8 _____ diccionario,

_____ 9 _____ globo y _____ 10 _____ tizas de colores. ¡También está

_____ 11 _____ cuaderno con _____ 12 _____ notas *(grades)* de todos

_____ 13 _____ estudiantes!

Q. ¿Cómo es la clase? Complete the following paragraph with an indefinite article **(un/una/unos/unas)** to tell what Señor González's classroom looks like.

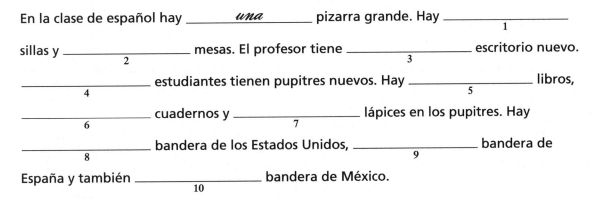

En la clase de español hay _____ *una* _____ pizarra grande. Hay _____ 1 _____

sillas y _____ 2 _____ mesas. El profesor tiene _____ 3 _____ escritorio nuevo.

_____ 4 _____ estudiantes tienen pupitres nuevos. Hay _____ 5 _____ libros,

_____ 6 _____ cuadernos y _____ 7 _____ lápices en los pupitres. Hay

_____ 8 _____ bandera de los Estados Unidos, _____ 9 _____ bandera de

España y también _____ 10 _____ bandera de México.

Descriptive adjectives (Lessons 1, 3, 5)

R. Toda la familia es ambiciosa. There are several traits that are common in Paulina's family. Paulina tells Jaime some of them. Jaime finds it hard to believe that everyone in the family possesses these traits and asks her about individuals. Write what Jaime says. (Watch the endings of the adjectives!)

Paulina: Nosotros somos morenos, generosos, amistosos, trabajadores y sinceros.

Jaime: *¿Tu padre es ambicioso, generoso, amistosos, trabajador y sincero?*

1. tu madre _____

2. tus hermanos _____

3. tus primas _____

4. tu prima Elena _____

5. tu abuelo _____

6. tus tías _____

7. tu primo Eduardo _____

8. tus tíos _____

S. Había (*There was*) un libro viejo. Paulina's mother likes to go to the flea market. One day she came home with the following items. Write the correct form of the adjective for each item.

Había unos libros (viejo) _____*viejos*_____ , una computadora (caro) _____ ,
1

unos lápices (barato) _____ , unas carteras (nuevo) _____ ,
2   3

una bandera (rojo) _____ , (blanco) _____ y (azul)
4   5

_____ , una papelera (gris) _____ , unas corbatas
6   7

(estrecho) _____ , un reloj (pequeño) _____ y unos cuadernos
8   9

(amarillo) _____ .
10

Possessive adjectives (Lessons 4, 6)

T. **¿De quién es?**   Rosita is helping Paulina clean the house. They find lots of clothes laying around, including some Paulina thinks may be hers. Paulina can't decide whose certain things are, first saying they belong to one, then the other. (Clarify using the **de** expression if necessary.)

Rosita: ¿Es tu gorro o el gorro de tu hermana?

Paulina: *Es mi gorro. No, es el gorro de ella.*

1.   Rosita: ¿Es mi suéter o el suéter de Carlota?

Paulina: _____

_____

2.   Rosita: ¿Son tus zapatos o los zapatos de tu mamá?

Paulina: _____

_____

3.   Rosita: ¿Son nuestras camisas o las camisas de Roberto y Tomás?

Paulina: _____

_____

4.   Rosita: ¿Es la chaqueta de tu mamá o la chaqueta de tu papá?

Paulina: _____

_____

5.   Rosita: ¿Es tu falda o la falda de Carlota?

Paulina: _____

_____

6.   Rosita: ¿Son los zapatos de Roberto o los zapatos de Eduardo?

Paulina: _____

_____

Placement of adjectives (Lesson 6)

U. Querido Raúl   Whenever Señor González intercepts a note, he reads it to the entire class. Rosita scrambles her sentences when she writes to Paulina so that if he intercepts it he won't be able to understand it. Here is a note he took from Rosita. Can you figure it out?

es chico guapo la Ramón el más de clase

_____Ramón es el chico más guapo de la clase._____

1. primo un Paulina mexicano tiene

_____

2. oscuro Su pardo tiene pelo primo

_____

3. morenos los Me gustan chicos

_____

4. ojos color café Los son el de claro

_____

5. chico guapo Es y un alto

_____

6. menores Eduardo hermanas tres tiene

_____

V. El cumpleaños de Rosita   For her birthday Rosita received many gifts. She tells Paulina about them, using all of the adjectives listed. Be sure the adjective agrees with the noun.

Recibí *(I received)* libros. (mucho/grande/interesante)

_____Recibí muchos libros interesantes y grandes._____

1. blusas (dos/bonito/rosado)

_____

2. pájaro (un/amarillo/pequeño)

_____

3. chocolates (un/francés/delicioso)

_____

4. discos (tres/popular/español)

_____

5. cartera (uno/grande/caro)

_____

Comparisons (Lessons 1, 2)

W. **¿Cómo son ellos?** Everyone is different. (As if you didn't already know that!) Write sentences showing how different people that Paulina knows compare.

Roberto es alto. Pablo es más alto.

Pablo es más alto que Roberto.

1. Mamá es amistosa. Papá es menos amistoso.

_____

2. Eduardo es delgado. Pablo es menos delgado.

_____

3. Pablo es joven. Eduardo es tan joven.

_____

4. Paulina es popular. Rosita es popular también.

_____

5. Salvador es simpático. Jaime es más simpático.

_____

6. Roberto es atlético. Papá es más atlético.

_____

X. ¿Y cómo son ellos? How do the following things compare to each other?

libro/computadora (caro)

Un libro es menos caro que una computadora.

1. un elefante/un pájaro (pesado)

   _____

2. un archivador/una mesa (alto)

   _____

3. un policía/un bombero (fuerte)

   _____

4. tu abuelo/tu abuela (canoso)

   _____

5. un ingeniero/un arquitecto (artístico)

   _____

Superlatives (Lesson 6)

Y. Mis ex-novios Jaime hasn't called for several days. Paulina is so angry she's thinking of him as an ex-boyfriend. She tells Eduardo who is the *least* . . . of her former boyfriends. (You remember—Diego, Jorge, and Jaime?) Help her by making some sentences with the descriptions below. (P.S. Guess who called that evening and apologized.)

Diego/Jorge/Jaime (simpático)

Diego es simpático. Jorge es menos simpático, pero Jaime es el menos simpático de todos mis ex-novios.

1. amistoso

   _____

   _____

2. generoso

_____

_____

3. guapo

_____

_____

4. fuerte

_____

_____

5. inteligente

_____

_____

6. ambicioso

_____

_____

7. trabajador

_____

_____

8. sincero

_____

_____

9. popular

_____

_____

Z. Mis amigos Paulina is telling her cousin Eduardo about her classmates. She tells him how they compare to each other and who is the *most . . .* of her friends.

Raúl/Manuel/Tomás (listo)

Raúl es listo. Manuel es más listo, pero Tomás es el más listo

de todos mis amigos.

1. Carmen/Susita/Eva (bonita)

_____

_____

2. Juan/Pablo/Jesús (guapo)

_____

_____

3. Silvia/Marisela/Felisa (inteligente)

_____

_____

4. Diego/Mauricio/Jerónimo (fuerte)

_____

_____

5. Carlos/Carlota/Inés y Elsa (popular)

_____

_____

⟐ Unidad III Lección 1 ⟐

Lo normal y lo anormal ¿Cómo estás?
Normal and not normal How are you?

VOCABULARIO   **El cuerpo** *The body*

A.   Identify the parts of the body.

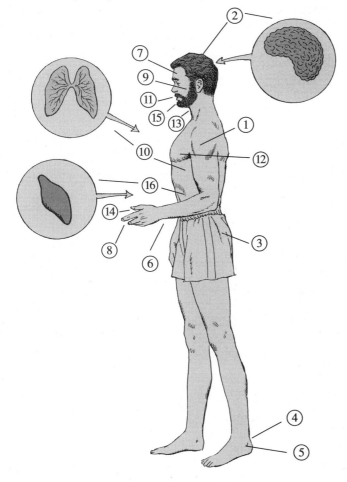

1. _____

2. _____

3. _____

4. _____

5. _____

6. _____

7. _____

8. _____

9. _____

10. _____

11. _____

12. _____

13. _____

14. _____

15. _____

16. _____

VOCABULARIO   Las enfermedades *Illnesses*

B. Fill in the patient's part of his conversation with the doctor.

MÉDICO   Buenos días. ¿Cómo está Ud. hoy?

PACIENTE   _____

MÉDICO   ¿Qué le duele?

PACIENTE   _____

MÉDICO   ¡Qué lástima! ¿Está Ud. agitado?

PACIENTE   _____

MÉDICO   ¿Está Ud. muy cansado?

PACIENTE   _____

MÉDICO   ¿Tiene Ud. fiebre o tos?

PACIENTE   _____

MÉDICO   Bueno, creo que Ud. tiene una infección del hígado. Aquí tiene un poco de medicina.

PACIENTE   _____

MÉDICO   Hasta luego.

PACIENTE   _____

ESTRUCTURA   *Use of articles with titles*

C. Señor Valdivia is at the bank with his wife and sees his co-worker Señor Ramírez. Complete the conversation with the correct forms of the article if one is needed.

SEÑOR VALDIVIA   Hola, _____ señor Ramírez. ¿Cómo está Ud.?

SEÑOR RAMÍREZ   Estoy bien, gracias. ¿Y Ud.? ¿Y ___*la*___ señora Valdivia?

SEÑOR VALDIVIA   Yo estoy bien, pero _____ señora Valdivia está un poco enferma.
                                                                   1

                    Ah, aquí está _____ señora Valdivia ahora. Paquita, éste es _____
                                                      2   3

                    señor Ramírez. _____ señor Ramírez es _____ contador en la
                                                 4   5

                    oficina donde trabajo.

SEÑORA VALDIVIA   Mucho gusto, _____ señor Ramírez.
                                                                   6

SEÑOR RAMÍREZ   El gusto es mío, _____ señora Valdivia. Creo que mi novia, _____
                                    7   8

Adela Fortuna, la conoce *(knows you)*.

SEÑORA VALDIVIA   ¿Adela Fortuna? Sí, _____ señorita Fortuna era mi profesora de
                                              9

matemáticas.

VOCABULARIO   **Estados emocionales y físicos con «estar»** *Emotional and physical states with* **estar**

D. Write a description of the person(s) in the blank. Use **está** or **están** with an adjective from
the lesson that matches the person(s) in number and gender.

Ellos están enamorados. _____

1. _____

2. _____

3. _____

4. _____

5. _____

6. _____

7. _____

8. _____

9. _____

10. _____

11. _____

12. _____

13. _____

ESTRUCTURA *The differences between* ser *and* estar

E. Write the correct form of **ser** or **estar** in the blank and then explain why you chose it.

El concierto _____*es*_____ en el parque.

Reason: _*I chose* ser *because a concert is an event that takes place.*_

1. El médico _____ en la oficina.

    Reason: _____

2. Carlos y su hermano _____ altos.

    Reason: _____

3. María y Luisa _____ nerviosas por el examen.

    Reason: _____

4. Alejandro _____ de Panamá.

    Reason: _____

5. Los muchachos _____ mexicanos.

    Reason: _____

6. La clase _____ a las diez.

    Reason: _____

7. Mi abuela _____ enferma.

    Reason: _____

8. Yo _____ aburrido(a).

    Reason: _____

9. ¿_____ Uds. listos?

    Reason: _____

ESTRUCTURA   Ser *vs.* estar *with adjectives*

F. Fill in the space with **es** or **está** according to the meaning of the sentence.

No me gusta esta sopa de pollo. ¡ _____ *Está* _____ fría!

1. Juan _____ aburrido cuando no tiene nada que hacer *(anything to do).*

2. La casa de mis primos _____ nueva.

3. Mi blusa favorita _____ vieja.

4. La clase _____ lista para el examen.

5. Víctor está con Dorotea. _____ juntos. *[Use the plural form of the verb.]*

6. Ese hombre tiene mucho dinero. _____ rico.

7. El hombre _____ casado con una mujer interesante.

8. Este programa de televisión _____ muy aburrido.

9. Hay solamente una persona en el cuarto. Ella _____ sola.

10. No puedo usar esta tiza. _____ rota.

11. Los animales no pueden escapar del parque zoológico. Todo el mundo

    _____ seguro.

12. Una persona que no tiene dinero _____ pobre.

13. El hombre tenía pulmonía *(pneumonia)* y ahora _____ muerto.

14. Esta muchacha es muy inteligente. _____ lista.

15. El niño tiene tres años. _____ muy joven.

16. El médico _____ seguro que tengo un catarro.

17. Mi amigo trabaja mucho en la escuela. _____ trabajador.

LEEMOS Y CONTAMOS

G. Sra. Molino is a hypochondriac who calls the doctor frequently. Read this conversation and answer the questions that follow.

SRA. MOLINO	Buenos días. Necesito hablar con el médico. Estoy muy enferma.
RECEPCIONISTA	Lo siento mucho, Sra. Molino, pero el doctor Salinas no está en la oficina ahora. Está en el hospital. Ud. puede hablar con la enfermera. Ella es muy lista y simpática.
SRA. MOLINO	Muy bien. ¿Dónde está la enfermera?
RECEPCIONISTA	Está aquí en la oficina.
SRA. MOLINO	Gracias. Ud. es muy amable.
ENFERMERA	Hola, Sra. Molino. ¿Qué tiene Ud. hoy?
SRA. MOLINO	No estoy bien. Creo que tengo una infección grave en los pulmones.
ENFERMERA	¿Tiene Ud. tos?
SRA. MOLINO	No, no tengo tos, pero me duele mucho el estómago.
ENFERMERA	¿Tiene Ud. fiebre?
SRA. MOLINO	Sí, creo que tengo una fiebre muy alta.
ENFERMERA	Si Ud. tiene fiebre y le duele el estómago, es probable que tenga gripe, no una infección grave en los pulmones. Y lo siento, pero no hay medicina para la gripe. Si Ud. no está mejor mañana, visite al médico. Él estará aquí mañana por la mañana.
SRA. MOLINO	Gracias, enfermera. Ya no estoy tan nerviosa y preocupada y me siento mucho mejor.
ENFERMERA	De nada, Sra. Molino. Adiós.

1. Why can't Sra. Molino talk to the doctor?

   _____

2. What does the receptionist suggest?

   _____

3. What symptoms does Sra. Molino have?

   _____

4. What does the nurse think is wrong with her?

_____

5. What does the nurse suggest she do?

_____

6. How is Sra. Molino now?

_____

H. Write a conversation between a sick patient and a doctor or nurse. Have the patient describe the symptoms in detail.

_____

_____

_____

_____

_____

_____

_____

_____

_____

_____

_____

_____

_____

Nombre _____

⇞ Unidad III Lección 2 ⇝

¿Dónde está...?
Where is . . .?

VOCABULARIO   **Preposiciones de ubicación** *Prepositions of location*
Las partes del aula *Parts of the classroom*

ESTRUCTURA   *Contraction of* de + el

A. There's been an invasion of butterflies in this classroom. Your job is to describe exactly where they are. You may want to review classroom objects in Unit I Tools.

Una mariposa está encima del escritorio.
_____

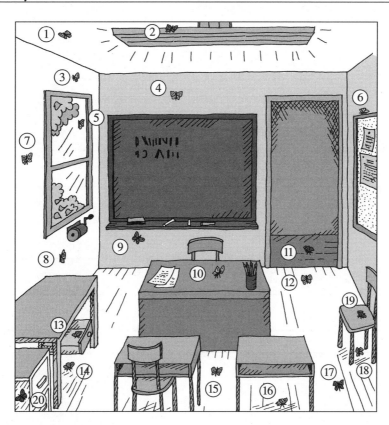

Nombre_____

1. _____
2. _____
3. _____
4. _____
5. _____
6. _____
7. _____
8. _____
9. _____
10. _____
11. _____
12. _____
13. _____
14. _____
15. _____
16. _____
17. _____
18. _____
19. _____
20. _____

ESTRUCTURA *Pronouns following prepositions*

B. Your Spanish-speaking classmate wants you to explain the new seating chart to him. Use the clues in English to guide your explanation.

Angélica *(in front of us)* _____*Angélica estará enfrente de nosotros.*_____

1. Carlos *(behind me)* _____

2. Juan *(with you and me)* _____

3. Mercedes *(next to them)* _____

4. Juanita *(near you)* _____

5. Roberto *(far from you all)* _____

6. Blanca *(to the right of me)* _____

7. Teresa *(to the left of us)* _____

8. Ana *(on the other side of you)* _____

9. Tomás *(between him and her)* _____

ESTRUCTURA *Two nouns together*

C. How do you express the following?

a gold ring

_____*un anillo de oro*_____

1. the Spanish class _____

2. a doctor's office _____

3. Miguel's friends _____

4. the students' teacher _____

5. a doghouse _____

6. his paper airplanes _____

VOCABULARIO   Lugares en la ciudad *Places in the city*

D. Be a tour guide. Identify twenty-five places in this city (refer to your textbook if necessary) and then describe where they are in relation to another landmark.

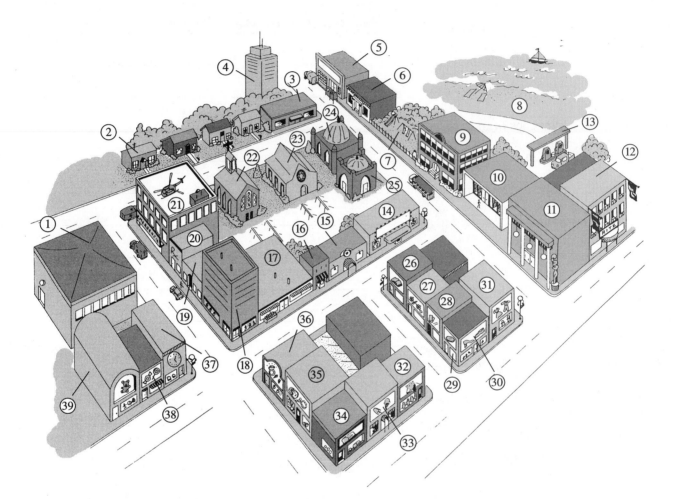

El consultorio del médico está al lado del hospital.

1. _____

2. _____

3. _____

4. _____

5. _____

6. _____

7. _____

8. _____

9. _____

10. _____

11. _____

12. _____

13. _____

14. _____

15. _____

16. _____

17. _____

18. _____

19. _____

20. _____

21. _____

22. _____

23. _____

24. _____

25. _____

E. Identify the objects on the left, then tell what store sells them.

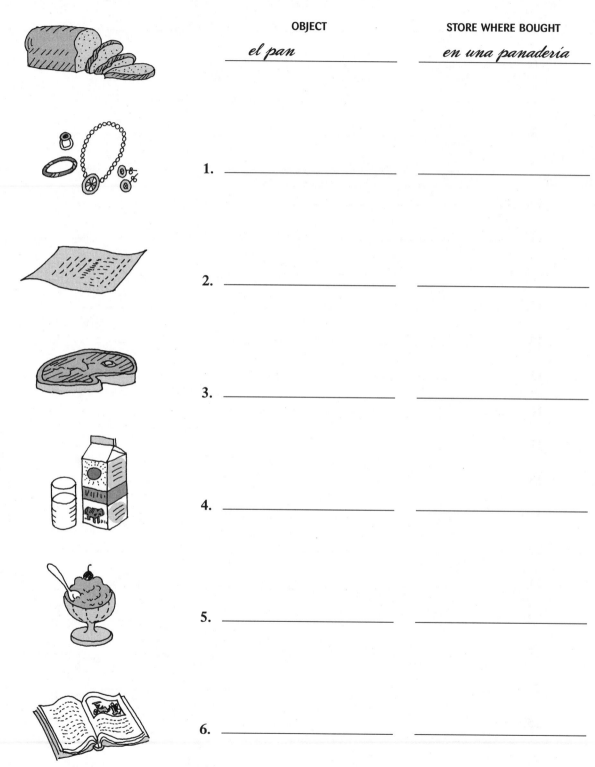

	OBJECT	STORE WHERE BOUGHT
	el pan	*en una panadería*
1.		
2.		
3.		
4.		
5.		
6.		

	OBJECT	STORE WHERE BOUGHT

7. _____ _____

8. _____ _____

9. _____ _____

10. _____ _____

11. _____ _____

12. _____ _____

13. _____ _____

LEEMOS Y CONTAMOS

F. Read the following description of Francisco's town and draw a map that corresponds to the description.

En el centro de mi ciudad hay un parque grande. Al oeste del parque está la iglesia. A la derecha de la iglesia está la escuela y a la izquierda está la biblioteca. Al lado de la biblioteca hay un museo. Cerca del parque hay un hotel y, más lejos, una playa bonita. En frente del parque hay un restaurante famoso y muy cerca está el almacén. Detrás del parque hay un cine y entre el cine y la estación de gasolina está el hospital. Es una ciudad interesante, ¿no?

Draw your map here:

DIVERSIÓN

On a separate sheet of paper, design your own city. Decide where to place all the buildings mentioned in the vocabulary list. Give your city a name.

⇒ Unidad III Lección 3 ⇐

Una lección de geografía
A geography lesson

VOCABULARIO **La geografía** *Geography*

A. Identify the countries and their capital cities in Spanish. Also identify geographic areas.

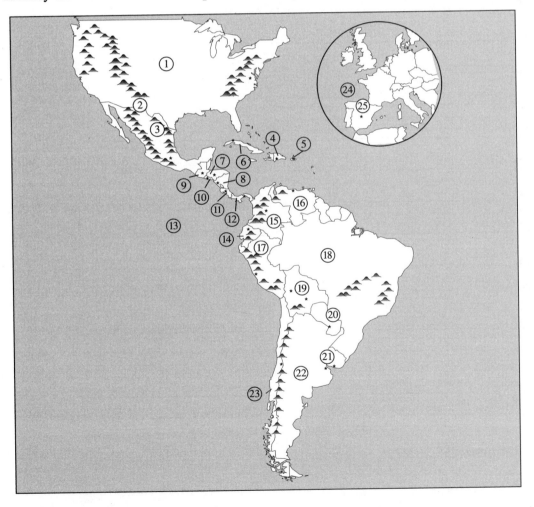

Nombre _____

1. _____
2. _____
3. _____
4. _____
5. _____
6. _____
7. _____
8. _____
9. _____
10. _____
11. _____
12. _____
13. _____
14. _____
15. _____
16. _____
17. _____
18. _____
19. _____
20. _____
21. _____
22. _____
23. _____
24. _____
25. _____

B. Identify the features on the map. Also identify the four directions on the compass.

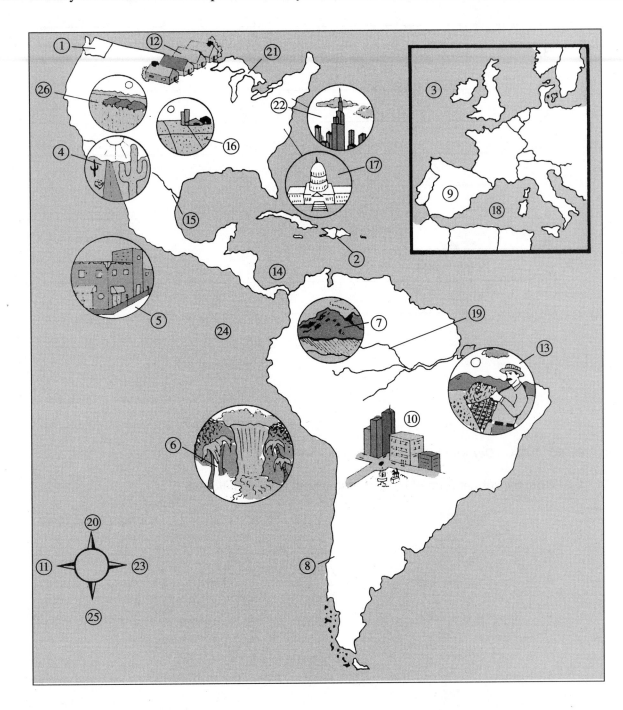

1. _____   14. _____

2. _____   15. _____

3. _____   16. _____

4. _____   17. _____

5. _____   18. _____

6. _____   19. _____

7. _____   20. _____

8. _____   21. _____

9. _____   22. _____

10. _____   23. _____

11. _____   24. _____

12. _____   25. _____

13. _____   26. _____

ESTRUCTURA   *Demonstrative adjectives*

C. Write the correct form of the demonstrative adjective indicated.

THIS/THESE	THAT/THOSE *[NEAR]*	THAT/THOSE *[OVER THERE]*
1. _____ ciudad	6. _____ islas	11. _____ llanos
2. _____ lagos	7. _____ desiertos	12. _____ selva
3. _____ río	8. _____ costa	13. _____ océano
4. _____ montañas	9. _____ país	14. _____ fronteras
5. _____ *(neutral)*	10. _____ *(neutral)*	15. _____ *(neutral)*

LEEMOS Y CONTAMOS

D. **Adivinanza** *Guessing game*   Guess the country that is described in the clue and then write the name of the country, its capital city, and the name for the inhabitants in the blanks.

Este país está en el hemisferio norte. Tiene costas en los océanos Atlántico y Pacífico. Tiene frontera con Canadá.

Ese país se llama ___*los Estados Unidos.*___

Su ciudad capital es ___*Washington, D. C.*___

Sus habitantes se llaman ___*estadounidenses.*___

1. Este país está en el centro del continente de la América del Sur. Tiene el lago navegable más alto del mundo. Tiene frontera con Brasil en el norte y con Argentina en el sur.

    Ese país se llama _____.

    Su ciudad capital es _____.

    Sus habitantes se llaman _____.

2. Este país tiene treinta y un estados y un distrito federal. Tiene frontera en el sur con Guatemala y Belize. Tiene dos costas, una en el Océano Pacífico y otra en el Océano Atlántico.

    Ese país se llama _____.

    Su ciudad capital es _____.

    Sus habitantes se llaman _____.

3. Este país está en la América Central y es muy pequeño. No tiene costa en el Océano Atlántico, sólo en el Pacífico. El nombre del país es similar al nombre de la capital.

    Ese país se llama _____.

    Su ciudad capital es _____.

    Sus habitantes se llaman _____.

4. Este país es muy montañoso. Tiene costas en el Océano Atlántico y en el Mar Mediterráneo. Tiene fronteras con Francia y Portugal.

    Ese país se llama _____.

    Su ciudad capital es _____.

    Sus habitantes se llaman _____.

E. Write a description for two Spanish-speaking countries other than the ones in Activity D. Each description should have at least three clues in it. Then write the answers in the blanks at the end of the description.

Country #1

_____

_____

_____

_____

Ese país se llama _____.

Su ciudad capital es _____.

Sus habitantes se llaman _____.

Country #2

_____

_____

_____

_____

Ese país se llama _____.

Su ciudad capital es _____.

Sus habitantes se llaman _____.

Nombre _____

✦ Unidad III Lección 4 ✦

¿Adónde vamos ahora?
Where are we going now?

ESTRUCTURA *The verb* **ir** *(to go)*

VOCABULARIO **Los medios de transporte** *Means of transportation*

A. Fill in the correct form of **ir** in the <u>future</u> and the mode of transportation illustrated to tell how these people will go on vacation.

Antonio _____*irá a pie.*_____

1. Ellos _____.

2. Nosotros _____.

3. Tú _____.

4. Maribel y su madre _____ .

5. Mi familia y yo _____ .

6. Ella _____ .

7. Uds. _____ .

8. Yo _____ .

9. Ud. _____ .

Nombre _____

VOCABULARIO Expresiones de tiempo *Time expressions*

ESTRUCTURA *Preterite and imperfect*

B. Fill in the blank with the correct form of **ir** in the <u>preterite</u> or <u>imperfect</u> depending on the time clue given.

De niño Alejandro ___*iba*_____ al parque todos los domingos.

1. Ayer nosotros _____ al cine a las 8:00.

2. La semana pasada Rosa y Amalia _____ a la tienda dos veces.

3. El año pasado Pablo y Raúl siempre _____ a la clase de español.

4. Hace un año yo _____ a un concierto con mi amiga.

5. Mi familia y yo _____ a la playa frecuentemente.

6. ¿Cuándo _____ tú a México?

7. Yo _____ a Chicago de vez en cuando.

8. Ramón nunca _____ a Puerto Rico.

9. ¿Tú _____ a la iglesia todas las semanas?

ESTRUCTURA *Contraction of* a + el

C. Juanita is writing a report on where people are going for vacation. Help her by filling in the correct form of **ir** in the <u>present</u> and **al** or **a la/los/las.**

Tomás y su familia ___*van al*_____ museo de arte.

1. Evangelina _____ playa.

2. Mi familia y yo _____ costa del Atlántico.

3. Tú _____ montañas.

4. Uds. _____ Río Grande.

5. Yo _____ llanos del oeste.

6. Miguel y Ricardo _____ desierto.

7. Ud. _____ selva tropical.

8. Él _____ lago.

ESTRUCTURA   Ir + a + *infinitive*

D. What are these people going to do on their vacation? Fill in the correct form of **ir** in the <u>present</u> plus **a** and an infinitive, which explains the action in the picture.

Mónica _____*va a descansar.*_____

1. Teodoro _____.

2. Isabel y Luisa _____.

3. Miguel _____.

4. Nosotros _____.

5. Yo _____.

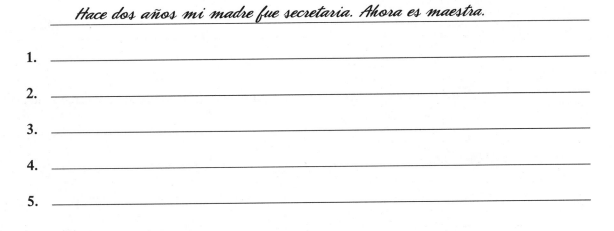

6. Tú _____ .

7. Paulina _____ .

8. Ellos _____ .

ESTRUCTURA   *Preterite of* **ser**

E. Tell about five people who have changed professions. (Review professions in Unit II Tools.)
Use time expressions and the preterite of **ser.**

  Hace dos años mi madre fue secretaria. Ahora es maestra.
_____

1. _____

2. _____

3. _____

4. _____

5. _____

LEEMOS Y CONTAMOS

F. Paulina told her class about one of her vacations in her public speaking class, but someone took bad notes during Paulina's report. Correct them by writing a statement that corresponds to the report.

Mi familia y yo siempre íbamos de vacaciones en el mes de agosto. Una vez fuimos al sur de California. Un día fui a nadar en la playa y todo fue muy bonito allí. Íbamos frecuentemente al centro a comer en los restaurantes. El fin de semana fuimos a Tijuana. Había muchos turistas que fueron allí a comprar ropa y otras cosas. Mi familia y yo fuimos a muchos lugares interesantes en ese viaje.

Paulina y su familia iban de vacaciones en el invierno.

No, ellos iban siempre en el mes de agosto.

1. Fueron a las montañas en el sur de España.

_____

2. Paulina iba a la playa todos los días.

_____

3. El fin de semana fueron al centro a comprar ropa.

_____

4. Iban a Tijuana frecuentemente.

_____

G. Now it's your turn to write about where you went on vacation. Write at least three sentences.

_____

_____

_____

_____

_____

_____

Nombre _____

⇻ Unidad III Lección 5 ⇺

¿Qué tenemos?
What do we have?

VOCABULARIO   **Los juguetes** *Toys*

A. Identify each toy in the picture.

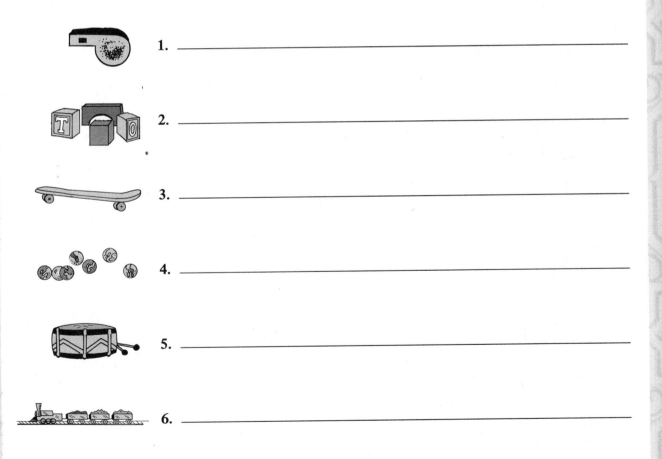

1. _____

2. _____

3. _____

4. _____

5. _____

6. _____

7. _____

8. _____

9. _____

10. _____

11. _____

12. _____

13. _____

14. _____

15. _____

16. _____

17. _____

18. _____

19. _____

20. _____

21. _____

22. _____

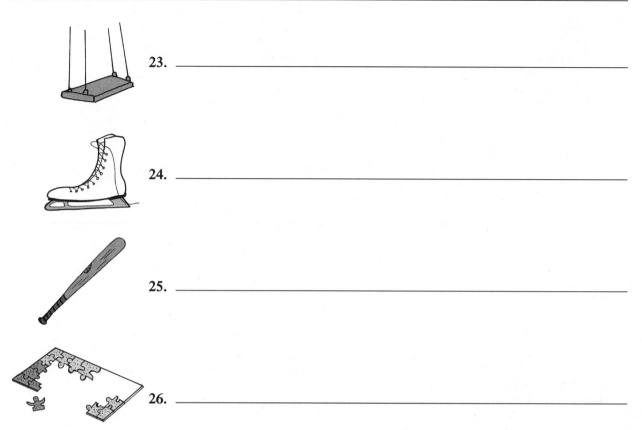

23. _____

24. _____

25. _____

26. _____

ESTRUCTURA   Tener *to have, Indefinite articles* (un/a/os/as) *with* tener, *Direct object pronouns*

B. Mention five toys that you had as a child and then tell whether or not you have them now by using an object pronoun. Use the <u>imperfect</u> and <u>present</u> tenses.

De niño yo tenía una carreta.   *La tengo todavía. / Ya no la tengo.*

1. _____   _____

2. _____   _____

3. _____   _____

4. _____   _____

5. _____   _____

Nombre _____

VOCABULARIO   Expresiones con tener   *Tener expressions*

C. Describe each illustration, using an appropriate **tener** expression.

1. _____

2. _____

3. _____

4. _____

5. _____

6. _____

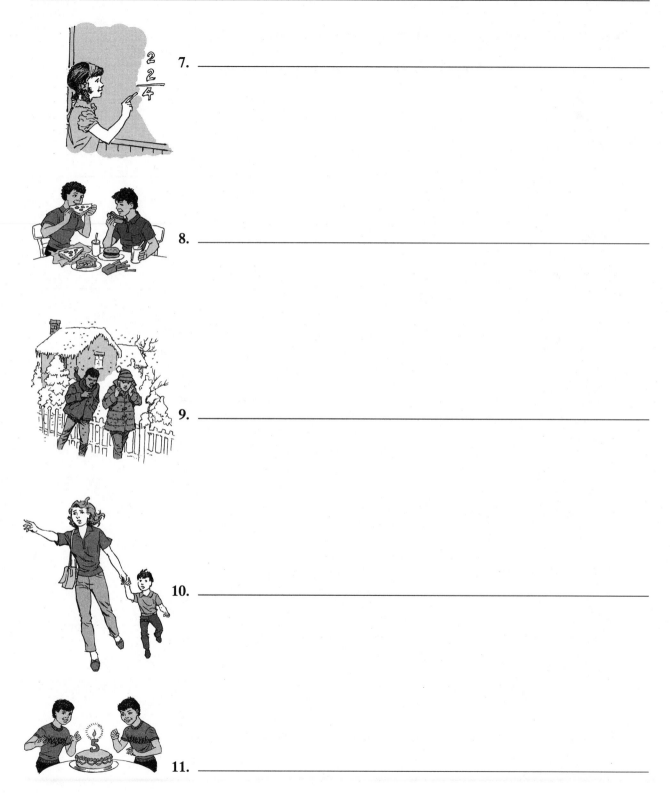

7. _____

8. _____

9. _____

10. _____

11. _____

ESTRUCTURA   Tener que + *infinitive*, Tener ganas de + *infinitive*

D. List four things that you will have to do to get ready for your vacation. Then list four things that you will feel like doing during your vacation. (See the Tools for Unit I if you need ideas for infinitives to use.)

TO GET READY FOR VACATION

Yo tendré que hablar con mis amigos.

1. _____

2. _____

3. _____

4. _____

ON VACATION

Yo tendré ganas de comer mucho.

1. _____

2. _____

3. _____

4. _____

ESTRUCTURA   *Preterite of* estar

E. Where were these people yesterday at 2:00 P.M.? (If you are not sure, guess.) Then tell where you were!

tu primo _*Mi primo estuvo en un restaurante.*_

1. tu amigo _____

2. tus padres _____

3. tu profesor(a) _____

4. tú y tus compañeros de clase (nosotros) _____

5. ¿Dónde estuviste tú? _____

LEEMOS Y CONTAMOS

F. Rosita is shopping for a birthday present for her niece. Here are some ads she found in the newspaper.

¡Cómprele uno nuevo!

En rojo vivo, con acentos en blanco y azul. Completamente ensamblado. Seguro y fácil de manejar.

Precio especial solamente
$49.95

La muñeca para crear memorias a su hijo o hija

Pelo lavable. Habla. Anda. Lleva la ropa de niña talla 2.

Ahora solamente
$29.98

UNA CASA DE MUÑECAS

Ideal para un niño o una niña de entre 4 y 12 años. Fabricada en plástico duro en varios colores brillantes. Completa con una familia de muñecas: padre, madre, hijo, hija e incluso perro y gato.

SOLAMENTE
$65.00

Help Rosita select her present. In English, tell why she should buy her niece one particular toy rather than the others.

Rosita should buy _____ because:

_____

_____

_____

_____

_____

G. Write a short paragraph telling what toys you had as a child, what toys you have now, and what toys you will have in the future.

_____

_____

_____

_____

_____

_____

D I V E R S I Ó N

Adivinanzas   Can you match the toys with the description? Write the
number of the description in the blank next to the toy you think it describes.

1. I get thrown around a lot. _____ el osito

2. I can take you for a ride but not go anywhere. _____ el columpio

3. I need a puff of air to make me grow. _____ el tambor

4. With your help I can talk and walk. _____ la carreta

5. The faster I go away, the quicker I return. _____ la pelota

6. If you beat me, I make a lot of noise. _____ los bloques

7. For me, three is better than two. _____ el globo

8. You can build a lot of things with me. _____ el títere

9. I'm not hard to bear because I'm so cute. _____ el caballo balancín

10. I have four wheels to carry you with. _____ el triciclo

Nombre _____

⊱ Unidad III   Lección 6 ⊰

¡Claro que me gustan los animales!
Of course I like animals!

VOCABULARIO   Los animales *Animals*

A. Identify each animal in the picture.

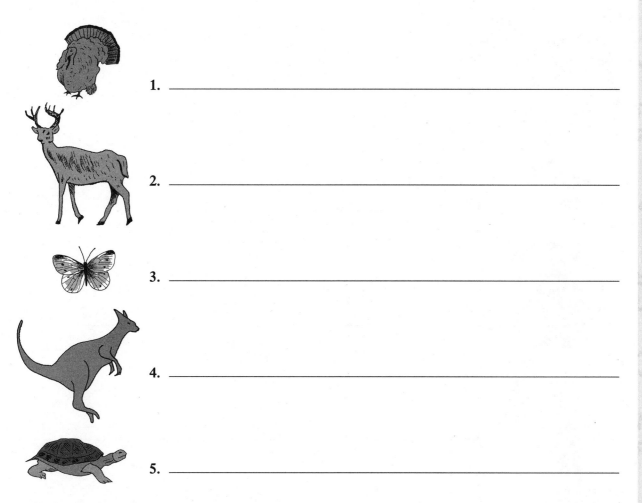

1. _____

2. _____

3. _____

4. _____

5. _____

6. _____

7. _____

8. _____

9. _____

10. _____

11. _____

12. _____

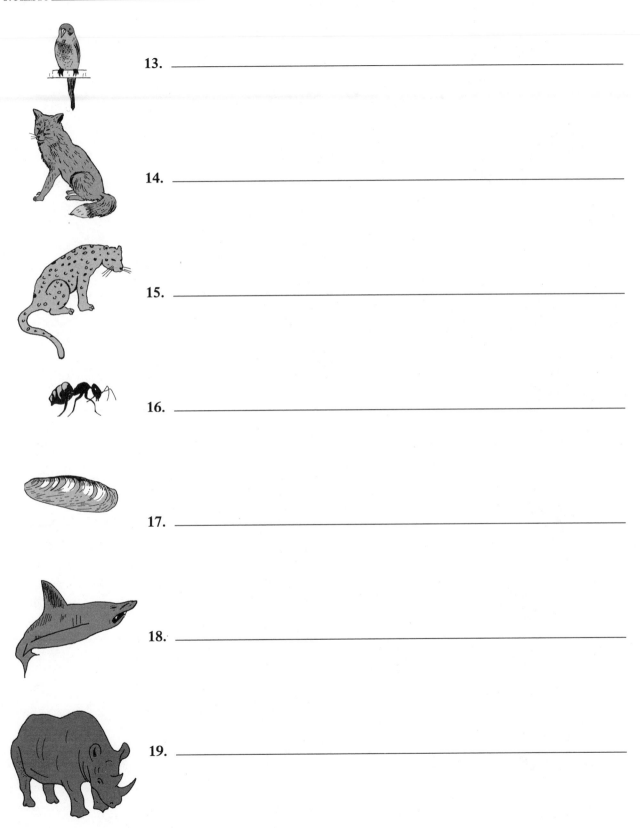

13. _____

14. _____

15. _____

16. _____

17. _____

18. _____

19. _____

20. _____

21. _____

22. _____

23. _____

24. _____

25. _____

26. _____

27. _____

28. _____

29. _____

30. _____

31. _____

32. _____

33. _____

ESTRUCTURA   **Gustar** *to be pleasing, to like*

B. Tell whether you liked or did not like the following as a child. (Use the <u>imperfect</u> tense.)
  ¿Te gustaban… ?

        los osos   *Sí, me gustaban los osos. /No, no me gustaban los osos.*

    1. las tortugas _____

    2. las serpientes _____

    3. los conejos _____

    4. las mariposas _____

    5. las arañas _____

ESTRUCTURA   *Indirect object pronouns, Clarification of indirect object pronouns*

C. The last time you went to the zoo or to a farm, which animals did the people with you like a lot? Write five sentences about five different animals. (Use the <u>preterite</u> tense.)

    A mi hermano le gustaron mucho las jirafas.

    1. _____

    2. _____

    3. _____

    4. _____

    5. _____

D. What would you and your friends like to do during the next vacation? Write five sentences about five different things you would like to do. (Use the <u>conditional</u> tense.)

    A mis amigos y a mí nos gustaría jugar béisbol.

    1. _____

    2. _____

    3. _____

    4. _____

    5. _____

LEEMOS Y CONTAMOS

E. Yolanda wrote a letter about her class field trip to the zoo. After reading her letter, tell who liked which animals there and why.

> Ayer estuvimos tres horas en el parque zoológico. Me gustaron especialmente los monos porque son como personas pequeñas. A Tomás le gustaron los leones y los tigres porque son animales fuertes y feroces. A Linda le gustaron los elefantes porque son grandes y simpáticos. Y a Tina le gustaron los conejos porque son como bebés. A Leonardo le gustaron las mariposas en los jardines porque tienen muchos colores y son muy bonitas. En realidad a mí me gustaron todos los animales en el parque excepto las serpientes. Nunca me gustaron las serpientes porque no tienen brazos ni patas y siempre están en sus estómagos.

Who liked or disliked which animals and why? Tell what you found out about each person.

TOMÁS _____He liked the lions and tigers because they are strong and ferocious._____

LINDA _____

_____

TINA _____

_____

LEONARDO _____

_____

YOLANDA _____

_____

F. Now it's your turn to write about the animals you like and do not like. If you can, tell why you like or dislike them. (Use the <u>present</u> tense.)

_____

_____

_____

_____

_____

DIVERSIÓN

Using the animals in this lesson, fill in the puzzle. One letter has been given to you for each animal. Use the clues to help you. Don't repeat any animals!

1. I hang around a lot. M _ _ _
2. My bark is worse than my bite. _ E _ _ _
3. Hear the roar? _ _ G _ _
4. Stubborn as a _____. _ U _ _ _
5. I'm your teddy. _ S _
6. I carry my house with me. _ _ _ T _ _ _
7. If I were a doctor, I'd be a quack. _ A _ _
8. I'll jump for you. _ _ N _
9. In the jungle I'm king. L _ _ _
10. I'm clever as a _____. _ O _ _ _
11. I have no legs. S _ _ _ _ _ _ _
12. If you had wings, you could fly like me. _ A _ _ _
13. Hippety hop and away I go. _ _ N _ _ _
14. I'm nuts for you. _ _ _ I _ _
15. I'm batty for you. M _ _ _ _ _ _ _
16. Thanks for giving. _ A _ _
17. I'm bigger than any one. _ L _ _ _ _ _ _
18. Polly wants a cracker. _ E _ _ _
19. Not a frog, but close. S _ _ _

Nombre _____

⇻ Unidad III Structure Review ⇺

PAULINA, SU FAMILIA Y SUS AMIGOS

Note: Review Tools section in the textbook at the beginning of Unit III before doing the activities in this Unit summary.

Ser *to be* **(Unit II), Estar** *to be (Lessons 1, 2, 3)*

A. Paulina desea dar una fiesta. *Paulina wants to give a party.* Paulina is trying to get her friends together for a last-minute birthday celebration for Salvador's birthday. She telephones Rosita to find out where everyone is. Complete the paragraph with the correct forms of **estar** in the <u>present</u> tense to help Rosita tell Paulina where everyone is.

Roberto _____*está*_____ en el cine. Pablo y Raúl _____ en el
1

supermercado. Tú _____ en la escuela, ¿no? Eduardo _____
2 3

en la biblioteca. Inés y Sean _____ en la farmacia. Mi hermano
4

_____ en la casa de Roberto. Carlota _____ en el consultorio
5 6

del médico. ¿Y yo? Yo _____ en mi alcoba.
7

B. No había fiesta para ti, Salvador, porque... *There wasn't a party for you, Salvador, because . . .* Complete the paragraph with the correct forms of **estar** in the <u>past</u> tense (**estaba** forms) to tell Salvador where everyone was when Paulina wanted to have the party.

Roberto _____*estaba*_____ en el cine. Pablo y Raúl _____ en el
1

supermercado. Eduardo _____ en la biblioteca. Inés y Sean
2

_____ en la farmacia. Carlota _____ en el consultorio del
3 4

médico y Rosita _____ en su alcoba. Fernando, el hermano de Rosita,
5

_____ en la casa de Roberto. Y yo _____ en la escuela.
6 7

C. No habrá fiesta para Paulina tampoco. *There won't be a party for Paulina either.* Everyone plans on traveling during the summer and won't be in town for Paulina's birthday. Complete the paragraph with the correct forms of **estar** in the <u>future</u> tense to tell where everyone will be.

Salvador _____*estará*_____ en Cuernavaca y Roberto _____1_____ en Chicago. Raúl

y su hermana Dorotea _____2_____ en Los Ángeles. Eduardo _____3_____ en

México. ¿Dónde _____4_____ tú en agosto? Yo _____5_____ en... Lo siento

mucho, *(I'm very sorry)* Paulina, nosotros no _____6_____ en la ciudad para tu

cumpleaños.

D. ¿Cómo están Uds.? *How are you?* A lot of Paulina's friends haven't been well lately. Complete the paragraph with the correct forms of **estar** to tell about it. Pay careful attention to the tense you use.

La semana pasada Salvador no _____*estaba*_____ bien, pero ahora _____*está*_____

mejor. Hoy Inés y Rosita _____1_____ enfermas, pero mañana _____2_____

mejor. Eduardo _____3_____ muy mal ayer, hoy _____4_____ un poco mejor,

y aún *(even)* Paulina _____5_____ así, así. ¿Cómo _____6_____ tú hoy?

Yo _____7_____ muy bien, gracias.

E. ¿Cómo están Uds.? *How are you?* Paulina and her friends are always busy. Use forms of **estar** and an adjective from the list below to tell how these people feel about what they have done today. (Pay careful attention to the agreement of the adjective.)

aburrido(a)	cansado(a)	enfermo(a)
feliz	nervioso(a)	triste
agitado(a)	contento(a)	enojado(a)
loco(a)	preocupado(a)	

Tuve un examen hoy. _____*Yo estoy preocupado.*_____

1. Inés tenía que ir al dentista.

_____

2. Eduardo perdió *(lost)* su libro nuevo.

_____

3. Jaime tuvo un accidente con su coche.

_____

4. Dorotea y Roberto tenían problemas con su tarea *(homework)*.

_____

5. Rosita recibió *(received)* un cheque de $100.

_____

6. Yo no dormí bien anoche.

_____

7. Nosotros no comprendemos la lección.

_____

8. Tú rompiste *(broke)* tu reloj caro.

_____

F. **¿Cómo es y cómo está? (Características y condiciones)** Paulina wants to tell us about her friends. Some things she tells us about use **ser** because she is describing their basic characteristics; others use **estar** because she is telling about their condition at the moment. Complete the paragraph with the correct forms of **ser** or **estar**.

Mis amigos _____*son*_____ amables y _____ muy atléticos. No
                                              1

_____ enfermos mucho. Ellos _____ contentos y solamente
         2   3

_____ tristes de vez en cuando *(once in a while)*. Ellos _____
         4   5

trabajadores y _____ muy listos. No _____ preocupados
                        6   7

cuando hay un examen. Y no _____ nerviosos tampoco *(either)*. Ellos
                                       8

_____ interesantes y yo no _____ aburrida cuando yo
         9   10

_____ con ellos. Nosotros _____ muy amistosos. Nosotros
         11   12

_____ locos por la música rock.
         13

Ir *to go (Lesson 4)*

G. **Adónde fueron todos?** *Where did everyone go?* It was a busy day for everyone yesterday. Everyone went somewhere after school. Help Paulina tell Eduardo where everyone went by completing the paragraph with the correct forms of **ir** in the <u>preterite</u> tense.

Ayer Dorotea _____*fue*_____ a la biblioteca y Salvador _____ al

supermercado. Inés y Rosita _____ al museo. Mamá y yo _____

a la ropería y después yo _____ a la zapatería y mamá _____ a

su oficina. ¿Adónde _____ tú?

H. **Los veranos cuando era niña** *Summers when I was a little girl* Paulina is telling her friends how she used to spend her summers. Help her by completing the paragraph with the correct forms of **ir** in the <u>imperfect</u> tense.

Cuando yo era niña, yo siempre _____*iba*_____ a México para visitar a mis abuelos.

Mi familia _____ conmigo y nosotros _____ por avión. Mis

hermanos _____ también a visitar a nuestros primos en el campo *(country)*,

pero yo nunca _____ con ellos. Todos los días, la cocinera *(cook)* y yo

_____ al mercado. ¿Adónde _____ Uds. durante el verano?

¿Adónde _____ tú, Rosita?

Ir a + *infinitive* *to be going to (do something) (Lesson 4)*

I. **¿Adónde van y qué van a hacer?** *Where are they going, and what are they going to do?* All of Paulina's friends and family have plans for the weekend. Can you guess who is going where and what he or she is going to do there? Write two sentences to tell where they are going and what they are going to do.

Rosita	al cine	ver una película

_____*Rosita va al cine. Va a ver una película.*_____

1. Rosita   a la fiesta   bailar y cantar

_____

2. Raúl y Pablo a la biblioteca buscar una revista (*magazine*)

_____

3. Dorotea al supermercado comprar la comida

_____

4. Eduardo y yo al almacén comprar un traje y una corbata

_____

5. Salvador al restaurante celebrar su cumpleaños

_____

6. Carlota a la piscina nadar

_____

7. Sus abuelos al hospital visitar a un amigo enfermo

_____

8. Sus padres al teatro mirar un espectáculo

_____

9. Nosotros al cine ver una película

_____

10. Yo a la casa de un amigo mirar sus fotos nuevas

_____

J. El fin de semana pasado *Last weekend* Rewrite the sentences in Activity I, telling where each of the people went last weekend.

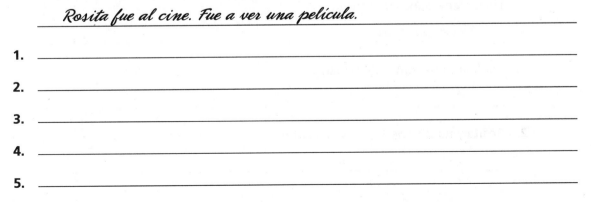

Rosita fue al cine. Fue a ver una película.

1. _____

2. _____

3. _____

4. _____

5. _____

6. _____

7. _____

8. _____

9. _____

10. _____

Tener *to have (Lesson 5)*

K. **¿Quién no tiene el Quijote?** *Who doesn't have the* **Quijote?** Rosita received two copies of *Don Quijote de la Mancha* (the famous book by Miguel de Cervantes Saavedra) for her birthday. She wants to give one of them to a friend. Paulina tells her who already has a copy. Complete the conversation with the correct forms of **tener** in the <u>present</u> tense.

PAULINA Tú _____*tienes*_____ dos ejemplares *(copies)* del **«Quijote».** ¿A quién le vas a dar

uno? Yo _____ un ejemplar. ¡Mis padres y yo _____
              1   2

tres ejemplares! Mi primo Eduardo _____ uno. Jaime y Salvador
                                                    3

_____ uno. Dorotea _____ uno también. Pero
          4   5

Fernando no _____ el «Quijote». Dorotea no lo _____
                              6   7

tampoco.

ROSITA Entonces, voy a dárselo *(to give it)* a Fernando.

Tener que + *infinitive to have to (do something),* **Tener ganas de +** *infinitive to feel like (doing something) (Lesson 5)*

L. **¡Qué suerte!** Everyone has to do something for the talent show. Fortunately, they can do things they feel like doing. Tell what each person has to do for the show.

Lucía tiene ganas de cantar.

    Tiene que cantar.

1. Paulina tiene ganas de bailar.

_____

2. Rosita y Raúl tienen ganas de cantar.

_____

3. Eduardo tiene ganas de contar chistes *(tell jokes).*

_____

4. Rosario tiene ganas de tocar el piano.

_____

5. Roberto y Sofía tienen ganas de presentar un mini-drama *(skit).*

_____

6. Fernando tiene ganas de hacer juegos malabares *(juggle).*

_____

7. Dorotea tiene ganas de vender billetes *(sell tickets).*

_____

8. Mónica tiene ganas de preparar los trajes *(costumes).*

_____

9. Javier tiene ganas de arreglar las luces *(arrange the lights).*

_____

10. Yo tengo ganas de asistir *(attend)* al espectáculo.

_____

11. ¿Qué tienes ganas de hacer?

_____

Tener *expressions (Lesson 5)*

M. **¿Qué le pasó a... ?** ***What happened to . . . ?*** Salvador is telling Paulina about some of the things that happened to their friends and how they felt about it. Review the **tener** expressions in the vocabulary and use them to fill in the blanks.

Luis deseaba una bebida.

Luis tiene sed. _____

1. Rosita celebró su cumpleaños. Había diez y seis velas *(candles)* en la torta porque ella

_____ diez y seis _____ .

2. Juan dice *(says)* que noventa menos diez son setenta. No _____

   _____ .

3. Juan dice que noventa menos diez son ochenta.

   Ahora _____ .

4. Hace mucho frío hoy. Emilia y Diego _____ .

5. Yo no dormí bien anoche *(last night)*. Yo _____ .

6. ¡Hay un león escapado del parque zoológico! Nosotros _____

   _____ .

7. No comimos el almuerzo *(lunch)* hoy. Ahora nosotros _____ .

8. Tú ganaste *(won)* la lotería. Tú _____ .

Imperfect and preterite (Lesson 4)

N. **Cuando yo era niño(a)...** ***When I was a child . . .*** Tell about five places you used to go when you were a child.

   De niño yo iba a la playa. _____

   _____

   _____

   _____

   _____

   _____

O. **La semana pasada** *Last week* Repeat the preceding exercise, but say that you went there last week.

   La semana pasada, yo fui a la playa. _____

   _____

   _____

P. La niñez de Paulina *Paulina's childhood* Paulina is telling Salvador about her childhood. Complete the paragraphs with the correct <u>imperfect</u> or <u>preterite</u> forms of **ir**. Watch for clues.

Cuando yo era niña _____*fui*_____ a México para visitar a mis abuelos. Todos los días

la cocinera *(cook)* _____*iba*_____ al mercado para comprar la comida y yo

_____ con ella. Nosotras _____ directamente a la carnicería
        1   2

(butcher shop) para comprar carne. Después _____ a la panadería para el
                                         3

pan y los postres y finalmente _____ a la frutería para comprar las frutas y
                                  4

las legumbres. Después _____ a la casa con toda la comida.
                        5

Un día mi prima Amalia _____ con nosotras. Amalia y yo _____
                        6   7

al parque para jugar mientras *(while)* la cocinera _____ a las tiendas.
                                      8

Yo _____ a jugar en los columpios *(swings)* y Amalia _____ a
         9   10

jugar en el tobogán *(slide)*. Después nosotros _____ a jugar en el cajón de arena
                                    11

(sandbox). La cocinera compró la comida y nosotras _____ a casa.
                                         12

El próximo día Amalia no _____ con nosotras y yo _____ con
                        13   14

la cocinera a las tiendas.

Q. La niñez de Paulina *Paulina's childhood* Paulina has another story about her childhood to tell Salvador. Complete the paragraphs with the correct forms of the indicated verbs. Watch for tense clues.

Cuando yo (tener) _____ doce años, siempre (ir) _____ al cine
                          1   2

con mi hermano Pablo y sus amigos. Ellos (ir) _____ todos los sábados.
                                         3

Nosotros (ir) _____ en el coche de mi madre.
                  4

Un día los amigos no (ir) _____5_____ al cine con nosotros. Mi hermano y yo (ir)

_____6_____ solos. Mi hermano (ir) _____7_____ a comprar los billetes.

—¿Por qué no (ir) _____8_____ tus amigos al cine?— le pregunté a mi hermano

(I asked my brother).—¿Por qué no (ir) _____9_____ nosotros con ellos? Mis

amigos (ir) _____10_____ a la playa esta semana. No (tener) _____11_____

ganas de ir al cine. Pero la próxima semana ellos (ir) _____12_____ al cine con

nosotros.

Después de *(After)* la película, mi hermano y yo (ir) _____13_____ a casa. Mi

hermano (tener) _____14_____ que estacionar el coche en el garaje. Cuando yo (ir)

_____15_____ a la sala todo (estar) _____16_____ preparado. (Ser)

_____17_____ el cumpleaños de mi hermano y todos sus amigos (ir)

_____18_____ a sorprenderle *(surprise him)* con una fiesta.

Pronouns following prepositions (Lesson 2)

R. **¿Dónde están mis amigos en el aula?** *Where are my classmates in the classroom?*
Here is a diagram of Paulina's classroom and the location of her friends. Help her tell where
they sit in relation to each other.

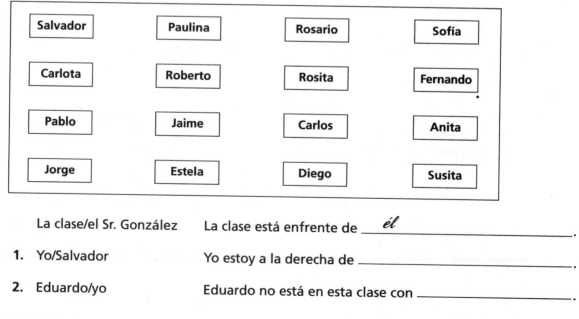

Salvador	Paulina	Rosario	Sofía
Carlota	Roberto	Rosita	Fernando
Pablo	Jaime	Carlos	Anita
Jorge	Estela	Diego	Susita

La clase/el Sr. González   La clase está enfrente de ___*él*_____.

1. Yo/Salvador   Yo estoy a la derecha de _____.

2. Eduardo/yo   Eduardo no está en esta clase con _____.

   3. Anita/Susita   Anita está delante de _____ .

   4. Jorge/Sofía y Rosario   Jorge está lejos de _____ .

   5. Jaime/Roberto y yo   Jaime está detrás de _____ .

   6. Roberto/Carlota y Rosita   Roberto está entre _____ .

Gustar *to please (I like, you like, etc.), Indirect object pronouns (to/for someone), Clarification of le/les, Emphasis of indirect object* (Lesson 6)

S. **En el parque zoológico *At the zoo***   Señor González is about to retire. Last week, as a special treat, he took the class on a field trip to the zoo. Everyone had a favorite animal they wanted to see. Tell what each person like most.

      Susita/los monos _____ *A Susita le gustaron más los monos.* _____

      yo/el léon _____ *A mí me gustó más el léon.* _____

   1. Paulina y Rosita/el elefante

      _____

   2. Fernando/los tigres

      _____

   3. yo/los pájaros

      _____

   4. Carlos y Carlota/los monos

      _____

   5. nosotros/los gorilas

      _____

   6. tú/el canguro *(kangaroo)*

      _____

   7. Dorotea y Jaime/los leones

      _____

   8. Raúl y tú/los osos *(bears)*

      _____

T. **¿Qué serviremos de postre?** *What shall we serve for dessert?* Everyone has a favorite dessert that they want to serve for Señor González's retirement party. Inés is telling Paulina about the problem they are having deciding what to serve. First tell what each person likes and then what they would like to serve. Be careful to use **gusta(n)** first, then **gustaría(n).**

Fernando/helado de chocolate _____*A Fernando le gusta el helado de chocolate.*_____

_____*Le gustaría servir el helado de chocolate en la fiesta.*_____

1. Rosita/la torta de vainilla _____

_____

2. Consuelo/los pasteles *(pastry)* franceses _____

_____

3. Roberto y Andrés/las frutas de Hawaii _____

_____

4. nosotros/la fruta fresca *(fresh)* _____

_____

5. yo/el helado de fresas *(strawberry)* _____

_____

6. tú/el helado de vainilla _____

_____

7. los otros *(other)* profesores/la torta de chocolate _____

_____

8. la clase del primer año *(first year)*/la torta de helado _____

_____

_____

U. Adiós a todo el mundo *Good-bye everyone* After the party, Señor González said a tearful good-bye to everyone. Tell to whom he said good-bye. Follow the example.

a mí _____*El señor González me dijo adiós.*_____

a ti _____*El señor González te dijo adiós.*_____

a sus amigos _____*El señor González les dijo adiós.*_____

1. a la clase de la primera hora

_____

2. a los otros profesores

_____

3. al director

_____

4. a los padres de sus estudiantes

_____

5. a los estudiantes

_____

6. a nosotros

_____

7. a la cocinera *(cook)*

_____

8. a la profesora de francés

_____

9. a mí

_____

10. a Uds.

_____

V. **Aquí tiene mi dirección** *Here is my address* In addition to saying good-bye, Señor González gave his address to everyone so they could keep in touch. Repeat Activity U but tell to whom he gave his address.

a mí ___*A mí me dio su dirección.*___

a ti ___*A tí te dio su dirección.*___

a sus amigos ___*A ellos les dio su dirección.*___

1. a la clase de la primera hora

_____

2. a los otros profesores

_____

3. al director

_____

4. a los padres de sus estudiantes

_____

5. a los estudiantes

_____

6. a nosotros

_____

7. a la cocinera *(cook)*

_____

8. a la profesora de francés

_____

9. a mí

_____

10. a Uds.

_____

Direct object pronouns, Position of object pronouns (Lesson 5)

W. **¿Qué hará con sus cosas?** *What will he do with his things?*   There were many things in the classroom that belonged to Señor González. Some of them he took **(llevó)** home. Others he left behind **(dejó)** in the classroom. Use the object pronoun and tell what he did with the following items.

la tiza   *La dejó en el aula.* _____

su suéter   *Lo llevó a casa.* _____

1. los papeles en el archivador

   _____

2. las banderas de México, de España y de Chile

   _____

3. la cinta de música de Julio Iglesias

   _____

4. la tiza colorada

   _____

5. el disco de bailes regionales

   _____

6. el diccionario inglés/español

   _____

7. los zapatos marrones

   _____

8. las cajas *(boxes)* de papel para la computadora

   _____

9. su cartera

   _____

X. **Muchas gracias a todos** *Thank-you, everyone*   Señor González received many gifts at his retirement party. Tell what he received **(recibió)** from everyone.

una planta exótica/Paulina y sus amigos

La recibió de Paulina y sus amigos.

1. un billete a México D.F./los otros profesores

_____

2. unas fotos de sus estudiantes/la clase de la primera hora

_____

3. un reloj de oro *(a gold watch)*/el director de la escuela

_____

4. un cheque de $150/los cocineros

_____

5. unas pelotas de golf *(golf balls)*/los estudiantes en la clase

_____

6. una cesta de frutas/los padres de sus estudiantes

_____

7. una corbata de seda *(silk)*/la señorita Blanco

_____

8. unos libros de aventura/las secretarias

_____

Contractions (Lessons 2, 4)

Y. **¿De quién es este coche?** *Whose car is this?* Salvador recognizes many of the cars in the school parking lot. One afternoon, walking with Rosita to his car, he tells her which car belongs to whom. Fill in the blanks with the correct form of **de** and the article.

rojo/el director — *El rojo es el coche del director.* _____

1. morado/el consejero _____

2. azul/la consejera _____

3. verde/los amigos de Paulina _____

4. negro/las cocineras _____

5. gris/la secretaria _____

6. pardo/el mesero _____

7. amarillo/los hermanos Ramírez _____

8. anaranjado/la señorita Blanco _____

Z. **Las aventuras de Carlota** *Carlota's adventures* Remember Carlota? She is Paulina's younger sister. Carlota had a busy day yesterday. Here is where she went. Insert **al, a la, a los, a las.**

Carlota fue _____ *a la* _____ escuela. Después, fue con unos amigos _____ *al* _____

restaurante chino en el centro. Después fue _____1_____ banco. Luego fue a visitar

_____2_____ amigos en casa de Jorge, entonces fue _____3_____ hospital

para visitar _____4_____ abuela. Cuando salió (*When she left*), fue

_____5_____ biblioteca y finalmente (*finally*) fue _____6_____ casa de su

amiga.

Demonstrative adjectives and pronouns (Lesson 3)

AA. **Ellos son hispanos. *They're Hispanic.*** There are a lot of students from Spanish-speaking countries at Paulina's school. She points out some of them. Complete the paragraph with the correct forms of *this/these.*

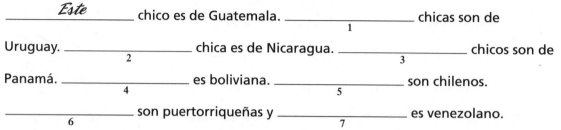

____*Este*____ chico es de Guatemala. _____ chicas son de
                                              1

Uruguay. _____ chica es de Nicaragua. _____ chicos son de
              2   3

Panamá. _____ es boliviana. _____ son chilenos.
             4   5

_____ son puertorriqueñas y _____ es venezolano.
      6   7

BB. **¿Cuál prefieres? *Which do you prefer?*** Paulina buys her gifts well in advance of when she needs them. But it's not easy for her to make up her mind when faced with choices. Help her choose some gifts for her friends' birthdays.

Para Rosita, ¿prefieres este libro de Cervantes o ese libro de Borges?

____*Prefiero ése de Borges.*_____

1. Para Salvador, ¿prefieres esa corbata roja o aquella corbata azul?

_____

2. Para Rosita, ¿prefieres aquella blusa de seda *(silk)* o esta blusa de algodón *(cotton)?*

_____

3. Para Fernando, ¿prefieres este disco mexicano o ese disco cubano?

_____

4. Para tu mamá, ¿prefieres este libro de poesía o aquel libro de recetas *(recipes)?*

_____

5. Para tu papá, ¿prefieres esos discos clásicos o aquellos discos de música rock?

_____

6. Para mí, ¿prefieres estas flores *(flowers)* o aquellas flores?

_____

7. Para la bebé, ¿prefieres esta muñeca *(doll)* morena o esa muñeca rubia?

_____

Noun modified by a noun = (noun) + de + (noun) (Lesson 2)

CC. **De quién es esto?** *Whose is this?* Several people left things behind when they left class late yesterday. Tell to whom each of these items belongs.

el bolígrafo/Salvador ___*Es el bolígrafo de Salvador.*___

el yoyo/Jaime ___*Es el yoyo de Jaime.*___

1. el libro/la chica nueva _____

2. la carta/el chico alto _____

3. la goma/Enrique _____

4. el cuaderno/Manuel _____

5. el peine *(comb)*/Gloria _____

DD. **Tienes que escoger.** *You have to choose.* Mamá went shopping with Carlota. Whatever they looked at came in several forms. Mamá let Carlota make the choice. What did Carlota choose?

una bufanda   seda/algodón/lana

___*Carlota escogió una bufanda de lana.*___

un anillo   oro/plata/cobre

___*Carlota escogió un anillo de plata.*___

1. un libro   aventura/recetas *(recipes)*/historia

_____

2. una blusa   algodón/poliéster/seda

_____

3. una mesa   madera *(wood)*/plástico/cristal *(glass)*

_____

4. una cartera   plástico/tela *(cloth)*/cuero *(leather)*

_____

El/la/los/las *with titles (Lesson 1)*

EE. **La profesora nueva *The new teacher*** Salvador wrote a short article for the school
newspaper about the new Spanish teacher who replaced Señor González when he retired.
Insert **el** or **la** before titles where necessary.

_____ señorita Carmen Blanco es nuestra nueva profesora de español. Ella es
    1

muy joven y bonita. _____ señorita Blanco es de Costa Rica. Era estudiante del
                        2

señor González cuando tenía diez y seis años. _____ señor González dice *(says)*
                                                   3

que _____ señorita Blanco era una estudiante buena. _____
      4   5

señor González dice también que ella es muy inteligente y simpática.

Cuando _____ señorita Blanco entró en *(came into)* la clase, _____
            6   7

señor González dijo *(said):* —Hola, _____ señorita Blanco. Estoy muy contento de
                                          8

verla a Ud. *(to see you)*—. Y ella respondió *(answered):* —Buenos días, _____ señor
                                                                              9

González. Estoy muy contenta de verlo a Ud. también.

Me gustaría tener a _____ señorita Blanco de profesora.
                        10

Nombre _____

❖ Unidad IV Lección 1 ❖

Vamos a dar una fiesta
Let's give a party

VOCABULARIO   **Una fiesta** *A party*

A. **Para preparar una fiesta**   Marta's family is preparing for her graduation party. Write at least five sentences which describe the activities in the drawing. (Refer to lesson vocabulary if necessary for ideas of what to say.)

Para preparar una fiesta...

La madre va a comprar refrescos.

1. _____

2. _____

3. _____

4. _____

5. _____

B. Para ir a una fiesta   Now the guests are going to go to the party. Describe the activity in each drawing that they are going to do. (Refer to lesson vocabulary if necessary for ideas of what to say.)

Para ir a una fiesta...

El muchacho va a aceptar la invitación. _____

1. _____

2. _____

3. _____

4. _____

C. **En la fiesta** Everyone is going to have a good time at the party. Describe at least ten activities in the drawing that they are going to do. (Refer to lesson vocabulary if necessary for ideas of what to say.)

En la fiesta...

Ellos van a charlar con sus amigos en la fiesta.
_____

1. _____

2. _____

3. _____

4. _____

5. _____

6. _____

7. _____

8. _____

9. _____

10. _____

ESTRUCTURA   *Regular -ar verb endings and personal a*

D. Paulina is making a list of who will do what for the party. Help her by writing a complete sentence with the cues given. Add the <u>future</u> ending that corresponds to the subject. Remember, if a person follows the verb, add a personal **a.**

Roberto y Ana/invitar/los vecinos

Roberto y Ana invitarán a los vecinos.

1. Simón/limpiar/la casa

_____

2. Tú/llamar/los amigos

_____

3. Tú y yo/comprar/los refrescos

_____

4. Yo/llevar/mi amiga Ana

_____

5. Uds./cocinar/la comida

_____

E. Lolita is talking to Celia on the telephone telling her what people are doing at the party. Help her by writing a complete sentence with the cues given. Be sure to drop the **-ar** from the verb and add the <u>present</u> ending that corresponds to the subject. Remember, if a person follows the verb, add a personal **a.**

1. Sandra y Paco/tocar/el piano

   _____

2. Marcos/saludar/los invitados

   _____

3. Roberto y David/mirar/la televisión

   _____

4. Yo/llevar/un suéter nuevo

   _____

5. Nosotros/escuchar/la música

   _____

F. The next day Lolita tells Consuelo (who wasn't at the party) what people did at the party. Write the same sentences as in Activity E, but use the <u>preterite</u> endings.

1. Sandra y Paco/tocar/el piano

   _____

2. Marcos/saludar/los invitados

   _____

3. Roberto y David/mirar/la televisión

   _____

4. Yo/llevar/un suéter nuevo

   _____

5. Nosotros/escuchar/la música

   _____

G. Paulina's father is telling her what he and her mother used to do at parties when they were young. Write the sentences using the <u>imperfect</u> tense endings. Remember, if a person follows the verb, add a personal **a.**

1. Yo siempre/invitar/tu madre

   _____

2. Ella frecuentemente/llevar/una blusa y falda

   _____

3. Nosotros generalmente/manejar/mi coche

   _____

4. Mis amigos siempre/invitar/muchas personas

   _____

5. Tú nunca/estar/en las fiestas

   _____

ESTRUCTURA   Dar *and direct object pronouns* (lo/la/los/las)

H. Here is a picture of some guests at the party and the gifts they gave. Write a sentence with the preterite of **dar** to explain what you see in the picture. Then repeat the sentence substituting an object pronoun **(lo, la, los, las)** for the thing or things they gave.

Ramón

Ramón dio unos casetes. Él los dio.

Beatriz   Silvia

1. _____

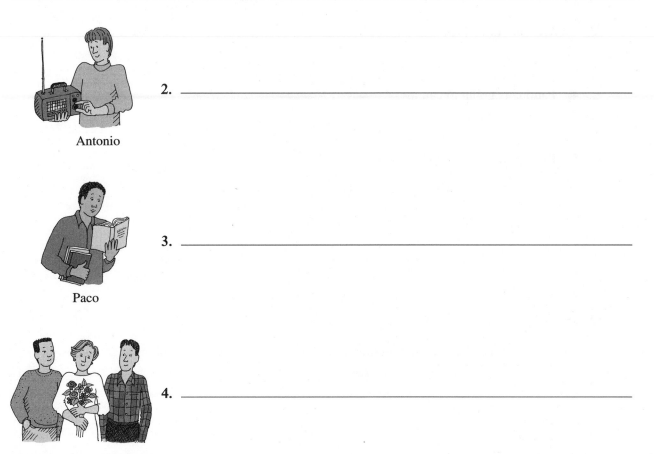

2. _____

Antonio

3. _____

Paco

4. _____

Fernando Isabel Teodoro

ESTRUCTURA   *Other direct object pronouns* **me/te/nos**

I. Write the following sentences in Spanish using the appropriate tense endings for the verbs and the direct object pronouns in the correct position.

José will invite us.

*José nos invitará.*_____

1. Did you visit them?

_____

2. My mother used to watch us.

_____

3. We want to help you.

_____

4. Paulina is going to call me.

_____

5. Expensive gifts? I always give them!

_____

6. Good parties? They used to give them.

_____

LEEMOS Y CONTAMOS

J. Paulina is writing to her uncle about the birthday party she had. Read her letter and then answer the questions that follow.

Querido tío Tomás:

Ayer tuve una fiesta de cumpleaños fantástica. Todos mis amigos estuvieron aquí. Invité a unos compañeros de escuela y vinieron unos vecinos también. (¡Los llamaba por teléfono por tres horas la semana pasada!) Mi padre me ayudó mucho con las preparaciones y mi madre cocinó una torta de cumpleaños. La comimos en la fiesta. Unos amigos nos ayudaron a limpiar la casa y mi madre y yo compramos toda la comida. Cuando comenzó la fiesta yo estaba tan cansada que descansaba y escuchaba la música mientras mis amigos bailaban y charlaban. Al fin de la fiesta les di las gracias a todos por los bonitos regalos y todos se fueron a casa. Ahora tenemos que lavar los platos y limpiar toda la casa. ¡Creo que mañana dormiré todo el día!

Hasta pronto,
Tu sobrina Paulina

1. Who was at the party?

   _____

2. What was Paulina doing for three hours last week?

   _____

3. Who helped prepare for the party and what did each person do?

   _____

4. What was Paulina doing at the party while her friends were dancing?

   _____

5. Now that the party is over, what do they have to do?

   _____

6. What is Paulina going to do tomorrow?

   _____

K. Now it's your turn to tell about a party you went to recently.

_____

_____

_____

_____

_____

_____

_____

_____

_____

_____

_____

DIVERSIÓN

Write the number of the sentence next to the person or persons doing the action. Can you think of other sentences to describe what is happening? You can add these at the end.

Antes de la fiesta

1. Adelina y su madre compraron la comida.
2. Su padre la ayudó con las decoraciones.
3. Adelina llamó a sus amigos por teléfono.
4. Adelina mandó las invitaciones.

En la fiesta

5. Adelina saludaba a los invitados.
6. Unos invitados bailaban.
7. Otros charlaban.
8. Otros miraban la televisión.
9. Un joven sacaba fotos.
10. Una muchacha tocaba la guitarra.
11. Unos cantaban con ella.

Después de la fiesta

12. Lavarán los platos.
13. Limpiarán la casa otra vez.
14. Adelina descansará mucho.

Nombre _____

¿Qué comes?
What do you eat?

VOCABULARIO   **La comida** _Food_

A. Identify the foods in the drawing on page 220 by writing the Spanish word in the correct category below. Write the number of the food after each word. You should identify at least ten foods in each category.

LAS LEGUMBRES Y LAS FRUTAS	LOS PRODUCTOS LÁCTEOS Y LAS BEBIDAS	LA CARNE Y LOS MARISCOS	PAN, CEREAL, POSTRE, ESPECIAS
el apio 60.			

B. List your favorite foods and beverages for each meal. Write at least five for each meal.

EL DESAYUNO	EL ALMUERZO	LA MERIENDA	LA CENA
café			
_____	_____	_____	_____
_____	_____	_____	_____
_____	_____	_____	_____
_____	_____	_____	_____
_____	_____	_____	_____
_____	_____	_____	_____
_____	_____	_____	_____

ESTRUCTURA   –Er *verb pattern*

C. Write the verb that describes the action next to each drawing.

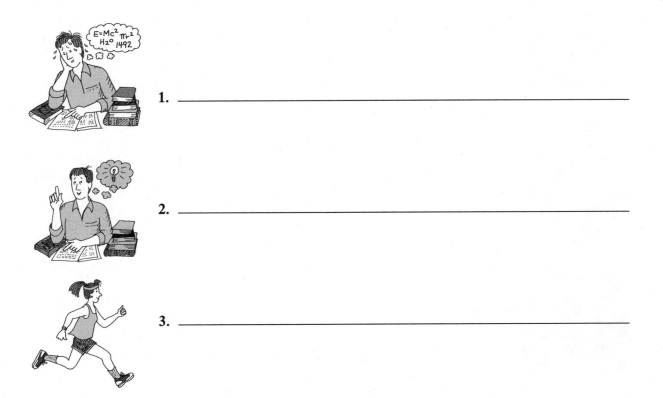

1. _____

2. _____

3. _____

4. _____

5. _____

6. _____

7. _____

8. _____

9. _____

D. Complete each of the following sentences with the correct form of the verb in the <u>present</u> tense.

Ellos (comer) ____*comen*____ a las dos.

1. Uds. (comprender) _____ el español.

2. Mi padre (correr) _____ todos los días.

3. Mi madre y yo (coser) _____ juntas.

4. Marisa no (vender) _____ sus libros.

5. Yo (leer) _____ muchos periódicos.

6. Tú (deber) _____ mucho dinero.

E. Complete each of the following sentences with the correct form of the verb in the <u>preterite</u> tense.

Mi amigo (romper) ____*rompió*____ la ventana.

1. Yo no (creer) _____ todo.

2. Carmen y Rosa (comer) _____ en la cafetería.

3. Tomás no (leer) _____ las lecciones.

4. Uds. (aprender) _____ mucho, ¿no?

5. Nosotros (vender) _____ la casa ayer.

6. ¿Tú no me (comprender) _____ ?

F. Complete each of the following sentences with the correct form of the verb in the <u>imperfect</u> tense.

De niño, él nunca (comer) ____*comía*____ las legumbres.

1. ¿Es verdad que tú siempre (creer) _____ todo?

2. Mis hermanos y yo (correr) _____ rápidamente.

3. El niño (aprender) _____ el alfabeto.

4. Las mujeres (coser) _____ las blusas.

5. Yo (vender) _____ las dulces.

6. ¿Ud. (leer) _____ en su alcoba?

ESTRUCTURA *Double-verb construction*

VOCABULARIO Verbos que combinan con el infinitivo *Verbs that combine with the infinitive*

G. Fill in the blank after the verb with a joining word *if needed*. If a joining word is *not* needed, leave it blank. Then tell what the sentence means in English.

Yo espero _____ aprender _____*a*_____ leer pronto.

___*I hope to learn to read soon.*___

1. Nosotros necesitamos _____ comer las legumbres.

   _____

2. Mis amigos insisten _____ beber refrescos.

   _____

3. Mañana nosotros tenemos _____ estudiar.

   _____

4. Yo siempre trataba _____ llegar a tiempo.

   _____

5. Te invito _____ ir conmigo a la fiesta.

   _____

6. Tú debes _____ ayudarla _____ preparar la comida.

   _____

7. Odio _____ comer las zanahorias.

   _____

8. El médico tiene ganas _____ leer el periódico.

   _____

9. Ellos acaban _____ aprender _____ esquiar.

   _____

ESTRUCTURA *Double object pronouns*

H. Rewrite the following sentences, replacing the nouns with the appropriate direct or indirect object pronouns. Then tell what each sentence means in English.

Juan le dio <u>las flores</u> a María.

Juan se las dio a María.

Juan gave them to María.

1. Nosotros les escribiremos <u>la carta</u> mañana.

_____

_____

2. La madre le leía <u>el libro</u> al niño.

_____

_____

3. Vamos a cantarte <u>una canción.</u>

_____

_____

4. Mis padres insisten en darme <u>unas lecciones de piano.</u>

_____

_____

5. Celia le vendió <u>su chaqueta</u> a Rosa.

_____

_____

LEEMOS Y CONTAMOS

I. Everyone has to do some things he or she does not want to do on the weekend. Read what Paulina's weekend will be like and answer the questions that follow.

Este fin de semana tengo ganas de ir al parque zoológico con mis amigos, pero mis abuelos nos invitaron a visitarlos y mis padres desean llevarme a su casa. No tengo ganas de ir porque mi abuela siempre insiste en darme guisantes para comer y odio comerlos. También me los da para llevar a casa. Voy a tratar de comerlos en su casa pero después tendré dolor de estómago. Y los guisantes que me da, se los daré al perro porque no tengo ganas de estar enferma dos veces.

1. Where does Paulina feel like going this weekend?

   _____

2. What do her parents want to do?

   _____

3. What does Paulina's grandmother always insist on?

   _____

4. Why doesn't Paulina like to eat peas?

   _____

5. What is she going to do with the peas her grandmother gives her? Why?

   _____

J. Complete the following sentences in Spanish.

Mis padres insisten en…

   Mis padres insisten en ir a la Florida para las vacaciones.

1. Yo tengo ganas de…

   _____

2. Yo tengo que…

   _____

3. Yo odio…

_____

4. Yo acabo de…

_____

5. En el futuro yo trataré de…

_____

6. Los estudiantes deben…

_____

7. Yo necesito…

_____

8. Yo les ayudo a mis padres a…

_____

9. En esta clase yo aprendí a…

_____

DIVERSIÓN

You have just opened a restaurant. What is it called? Make a menu for your restaurant. Be sure to include a section of appetizers **(entremeses),** dinners **(cenas),** soups **(sopas),** desserts **(postres),** and drinks **(bebidas).**

Menú

Nombre _____

✦ Unidad IV Lección 3 ✦

¿Dónde vives? ¿De dónde vienes?
Where do you live? Where are you coming from?

VOCABULARIO   **¿Dónde vives?** _Where do you live?_

A. First write how you express each sentence in English. Then write the name of the person under the drawing that corresponds to the description on page 230 of where he or she lives.

> TINA   Yo vivo en una casa moderna en un barrio seguro en las afueras.
>
> _I live in a modern house in a safe neighborhood in the suburbs._

1. MARISELA   Yo vivo en un apartamento en el quinto piso de un rascacielos.

_____

_____

2. SRA. MORENO   Yo vivo en un condominio en un barrio tranquilo en las afueras de la ciudad.

_____

_____

3. PEDRO   Yo vivo en un apartamento nuevo en una calle concurrida y ruidosa en la ciudad.

_____

_____

4. RAMÓN   Yo vivo en una casa vieja, en una granja en el campo a cien millas de la ciudad.

_____

_____

5. ADELITA   Yo vivo en un apartamento viejo, en una calle sucia y peligrosa en el centro de la ciudad.

_____

_____

Tina _____

_____

_____

_____

_____

_____

B. Label the floors of this skyscraper. Don't forget the basement and ground floor.

1. _____

2. _____

3. _____

4. _____

5. _____

6. _____

7. _____

8. _____

9. _____

10. _____

11. _____

12. _____

13. _____

ESTRUCTURA *Verbs that end in* -ir

C. Give the English equivalent of the following sentences. Pay particular attention to the time (tense) of the verb.

La madre sufría mucho.

_*The mother used to suffer a lot.*_____

1. Nosotros escribimos muchas cartas.

   _____

2. Marcos y Angelina recibieron muchos regalos.

   _____

3. Mis padres insisten en asistir a la iglesia.

   _____

4. Los niños subirán al autobús.

   _____

5. El muchacho abrió la ventana.

   _____

6. Los señores Galdós discuten la comida.

   _____

ESTRUCTURA **Venir** *to come*

D. Does every member always come to your Spanish Club meeting? Let's see who the club president thinks will come. Complete the sentences with the correct forms of **venir** in the <u>future</u> tense.

Mi amigo Ramón _____*vendrá*_____ a la reunión.

1. Magdalena y Selena _____ si tienen tiempo.

2. Toño _____ si hay buena comida.

3. Tú _____ también, ¿no?

4. Yo _____ por seguro.

5. Todos nosotros _____ temprano.

E. Now let's see who actually came to the meeting. Complete the sentences with the correct forms of **venir** in the <u>preterite</u> tense.

Mi amigo Ramón no _____*vino*_____ a la reunión.

1. Magdalena y Selena _____ porque sí tenían tiempo.

2. Toño _____ porque había buena comida.

3. Tú _____ también, ¿no?

4. Yo _____ por seguro.

5. No todos nosotros _____ temprano.

F. The Spanish Club meeting is held in a Mexican restaurant on the weekend. Let's see where the members come from. Complete the sentences with the correct forms of **venir** in the <u>present</u> tense.

Mi amigo Ramón _____*viene*_____ de su casa.

1. Magdalena y Selena _____ de su partido de tenis.

2. Toño _____ después de su desayuno.

3. ¿De dónde _____ tú?

4. Yo _____ del trabajo.

5. Todos nosotros _____ de alguna actividad.

LEEMOS Y CONTAMOS

G. Read about Catalina's home situation and answer the questions that follow.

Antes vivíamos en un barrio con muchos problemas. El año pasado mis padres, mi hermano y yo discutimos irnos a un nuevo barrio. Mi padre deseaba vivir en una casa vieja en el campo, pero mi madre no deseaba sufrir con las moscas. Mi madre insistía en vivir en un apartamento nuevo en una calle tranquila en las afueras de la ciudad, pero yo no deseaba viajar diez millas para asistir a mi escuela. Yo prefería vivir en una calle concurrida cerca del centro, pero mi padre no deseaba sufrir con el ruido. Mi hermano deseaba vivir en un rascacielos en el centro, pero nadie deseaba subir quince pisos. El resultado fue que nosotros decidimos vivir en el mismo barrio, en la misma casa con los mismos problemas.

1. What did Catalina's family discuss last year? Why?

_____

2. Where did her father want to live?

_____

3. Why did her mother object?

_____

4. Where did her mother want to live?

_____

5. Why did Catalina object?

_____

6. Where did Catalina want to live?

_____

7. Why did her father object?

_____

8. Where did her brother want to live?

_____

9. Who objected to that plan and why?

_____

10. What did they decide to do then?

_____

H. Write about a neighborhood where you live, used to live, or will live.

_____

_____

_____

_____

DIVERSIÓN

On a separate sheet of paper, draw a map showing the way from your home to your school. Put in the main streets and the other streets near both your school and home. Locate some of the important buildings. Write directions in Spanish for getting from one place to the other.

Nombre _____

Mi día en la escuela
My day at school

VOCABULARIO   **En la escuela** _In school_

A. In the space provided, write the Spanish equivalent for each of the following. The first one has been done for you.

1. ARTS _Las artes_
2. art _____
3. drama _____
4. music _____
5. SCIENCES _____
6. biology _____
7. physics _____
8. chemistry _____
9. SOCIAL SCIENCES _____
10. geography _____
11. history _____
12. psychology _____
13. BUSINESS _____
14. computer science _____
15. keyboarding _____

16. shorthand _____
17. FOREIGN LANGUAGES _____
18. German _____
19. Chinese _____
20. Spanish _____
21. French _____
22. Italian _____
23. Japanese _____
24. Russian _____
25. MATH _____
26. algebra _____
27. calculus _____
28. geometry _____
29. trigonometry _____
30. OTHER SUBJECTS _____

31. physical education _____
32. elementary school _____
33. secondary school _____
34. college _____
35. private high school _____

36. freshman _____
37. sophomore _____
38. junior _____
39. senior _____
40. first grade _____

VOCABULARIO   Lo que hacemos en la escuela *What we do in school*

B. Write a sentence that describes what you think the people in each drawing are doing. Remember to put the correct personal ending on the verb. (There may be more than one correct answer.)

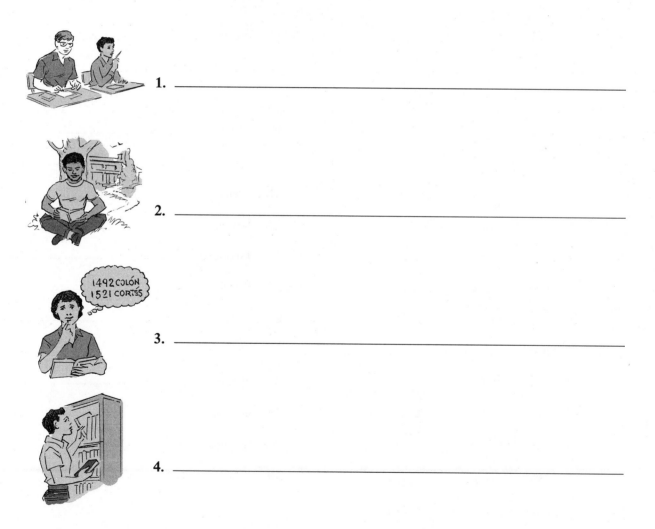

1. _____

2. _____

3. _____

4. _____

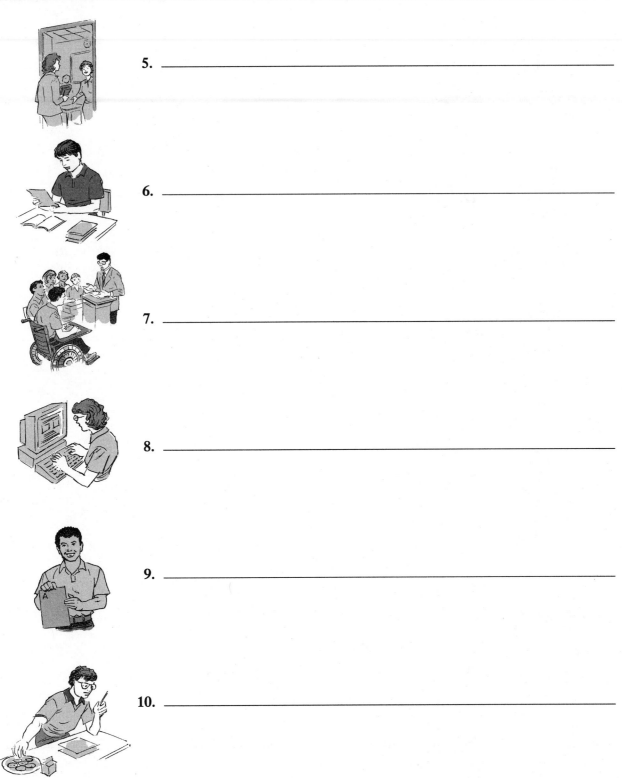

5. _____

6. _____

7. _____

8. _____

9. _____

10. _____

11. _____

12. _____

13. _____

14. _____

15. _____

16. _____

ESTRUCTURA   "Boot verbs" (Present tense of stem-changing verbs)

C. Complete the sentence with the correct form of the <u>present</u> tense of the verb in parentheses.

Algunos niños (preferir) _____ *prefieren* _____ jugar.

1. La madre (servir) _____ algo bueno.

2. Nadie (recordar) _____ su cumpleaños.

3. Nosotros no (dormir) _____ mucho.

4. Las blusas (costar) _____ $5.00.

5. ¿(Poder) _____ tú ayudarme ahora?

6. Los mecánicos (volver) _____ mañana.

7. El profesor siempre (repetir) _____ las palabras.

8. ¿Uds. nunca (cerrar) _____ la puerta?

9. Nosotros (querer) _____ descansar.

10. La muchacha (pedir) _____ otro vaso de leche.

11. El perro (seguir) _____ al niño.

12. Yo (pensar) _____ que es correcto.

13. Los estudiantes (comenzar) _____ a comer.

14. ¿Dónde (preferir) _____ Uds. estudiar?

15. Mi padre siempre (perder) _____ las llaves.

16. Nosotros (almorzar) _____ a las doce.

17. Los niños (jugar) _____ en el parque.

18. Las cucarachas no (morir) _____ fácilmente.

19. Celia generalmente (dormir) _____ bien.

20. Sandra y yo (preferir) _____ café.

21. Yo siempre (seguir) _____ las instrucciones.

ESTRUCTURA   *The meanings of* pensar

D. Read the following conversation between Julio and Luis and fill in each blank with **de, en,** or **que,** depending on the meaning of the sentence. (The English equivalent is provided.) Leave blank if nothing is needed.

JULIO   ¿Qué piensas _____ estudiar juntos?
        $\overline{\qquad 1 \qquad}$

   (What do you think about studying together?)

LUIS   Pienso _____ es una buena idea.
       $\overline{\qquad 2 \qquad}$

   (I think it's a good idea.)

JULIO   Pienso _____ matemáticas.
        $\overline{\qquad 3 \qquad}$

   (I plan to study math.)

LUIS   ¿ _____ qué piensas cuando no estás estudiando?
       $\overline{\qquad 4 \qquad}$

   (What do you think about when you're not studying?)

JULIO   Pienso _____ las vacaciones, ¡por supuesto!
        $\overline{\qquad 5 \qquad}$

   (I think about vacation, of course!)

LUIS   ¿Qué piensas _____ la nueva estudiante?
       $\overline{\qquad 6 \qquad}$

   (What do you think about the new student?)

JULIO   Pienso _____ es muy simpática.
        $\overline{\qquad 7 \qquad}$

   (I think she's very nice.)

LUIS   Yo pienso _____ ella mucho.
       $\overline{\qquad 8 \qquad}$

   (I think about her a lot.)

JULIO   ¿Sabes lo que pienso _____ eso?
        $\overline{\qquad 9 \qquad}$

   (You know what I think about that?)

LUIS   Pienso _____ estás enamorado de ella.
       $\overline{\qquad 10 \qquad}$

   (I think you're in love with her.)

ESTRUCTURA   *"Slipper verbs" (Preterite tense of stem-changing verbs)*

E. Complete each sentence with the correct form of the <u>preterite</u> tense of the verb in parentheses. Then tell what the sentence means. (Be careful, some forms will not require a stem change.)

Esta mañana mis padres (dormir) _____ *durmieron* _____ tarde.

_____ *This morning my parents slept late.* _____.

1. A las 9:00 el invitado (pedir) _____ algo para comer.

   _____

2. En el pasado, ellos siempre (seguir) _____ las instrucciones.

   _____

3. Anoche yo (dormir) _____ ocho horas.

   _____

4. El estudiante (repetir) _____ la lección.

   _____

5. La camarera nos (servir) _____ la comida rápidamente.

   _____

6. Mi perro (morir) _____ ayer.

   _____

7. La semana pasada Uds. (preferir) _____ llegar tarde, ¿no?

   _____

8. ¿Tú nunca (pedir) _____ ayuda?

   _____

9. El policía (seguir) _____ a algunos hombres al parque.

   _____

ESTRUCTURA *Using adjectives without a noun*

F. Give the Spanish equivalent of the following sentences.

The fun part is eating apples. I like the green ones.

Lo divertido es comer manzanas. Me gustan las verdes.

1. The important thing is to arrive on time.

2. Books? I like the short ones.

3. Cars? We prefer the expensive ones.

4. The good part is the food.

5. The difficult part is the verbs.

VOCABULARIO *Neutral and negative words*

ESTRUCTURA *Using negative words*

G. Rewrite the following sentences in the negative by changing the underlined words to the negative and adding **no** if needed. Then tell what the sentence means in English.

Yo compré <u>algo</u> para <u>alguien también</u>.

Yo no compré nada para nadie tampoco.

I didn't buy anything for anybody either.

1. Mi padre <u>siempre</u> bebe <u>o</u> té <u>o</u> café.

2. <u>Algunos</u> chicos escribieron <u>algo</u>.

_____

_____

3. Yo veo a <u>alguien</u> en la casa <u>también</u>.

_____

_____

LEEMOS Y CONTAMOS

H. Read what the following students say about their classes.

RENALDO   Rosa, yo soy estudiante de primer año en esta escuela secundaria y quiero saber cómo son las clases aquí. ¿Qué pasó en tus clases el año pasado?

ROSA   El año pasado yo tomé una clase de biología. Lo malo fue tener que disecar ranas. Algunos estudiantes le pidieron ayuda al profesor, pero yo nunca le pedí nada. Sólo pensé en las ranas que murieron y cuando el profesor me sirvió una rana yo la seguí cuando salió de la clase por la ventana. Claro, suspendí la prueba esa semana, pero afortunadamente aprobé el examen final porque tomé buenos apuntes y escribí toda la tarea en la computadora.

RENALDO   No me molesta nada tener que disecar ranas, así que pienso que no habrá ningún problema. Lo difícil para mí son las matemáticas. Puedo sumar y restar sin dificultad pero multiplicar y dividir es algo diferente. Y tú, ¿prefieres las clases elementales de matemáticas o las avanzadas?

ROSA   Bueno, Renaldo, la verdad es que sé calcular perfectamente bien, así que estudié cálculo y trigonometría. Saqué una *A* en todos los exámenes.

RENALDO   ¡Dios mío, Rosa! Eres un verdadero genio. Si puedo pedirte ayuda con las matemáticas, yo te puedo ayudar con las investigaciones de biología. ¿Está bien?

ROSA   Sí, Renaldo, ¡trabajaremos juntos y aprenderemos juntos también!

Answer the following questions about Rosa and Renaldo.

1. What grade is Renaldo in?

_____

2. What does he want to know about?

_____

3. What was the bad part about Rosa's biology class?

_____

4. What happened when the instructor gave her a frog to dissect?

_____

5. What grade did she get in biology?

_____

6. What is the difficult thing in school for Renaldo?

_____

7. How did Rosa do in math?

_____

8. What is Renaldo's reaction?

_____

9. What are Rosa and Renaldo going to do in the future?

_____

I. Now it's your turn to tell about your experiences in your classes.

_____

_____

_____

_____

_____

_____

_____

_____

_____

_____

Nombre _____

⇉ Unidad IV Lección 5 ⇇

Un día en mi vida
A day in my life

ESTRUCTURA   *Reflexive (-self) pronouns, Position of reflexive pronouns*

A. Give the Spanish equivalent of each sentence, using the appropriate *-self* pronoun. The Spanish verbs are provided.

We need to give ourselves credit.   **(necesitar, dar)**

Necesitamos darnos crédito. / Nos necesitamos dar crédito.

1. We see ourselves in the photo.   **(ver)**

   _____

2. Carmela talks to herself.   **(hablar)**

   _____

3. I'm going to wash myself now.   **(ir, lavar)**

   _____

4. Do you understand yourself?   **(comprender)**

   _____

5. They want to look at themselves in the mirror.   **(querer, mirar)**

   _____

ESTRUCTURA   *Each other* = nos *and* se

B. Give the Spanish equivalent of each sentence.

1. They talk to each other a lot.   **(hablar)**

   _____

2. We need each other.   **(necesitar)**

   _____

3. Raúl and Luis are going to see each other.   **(ir, ver)**

   _____

4. We want to get to know each other.   **(querer, conocer)**

   _____

VOCABULARIO   **La rutina diaria** *Daily routine*

ESTRUCTURA   *Reflexive verbs*

C. Describe what the people in the drawing are doing, using one of the reflexive verbs. There may be more than one possible answer. Be careful to use the correct ending of the verb and to put the *–self* pronoun first.

1. _____

2. _____

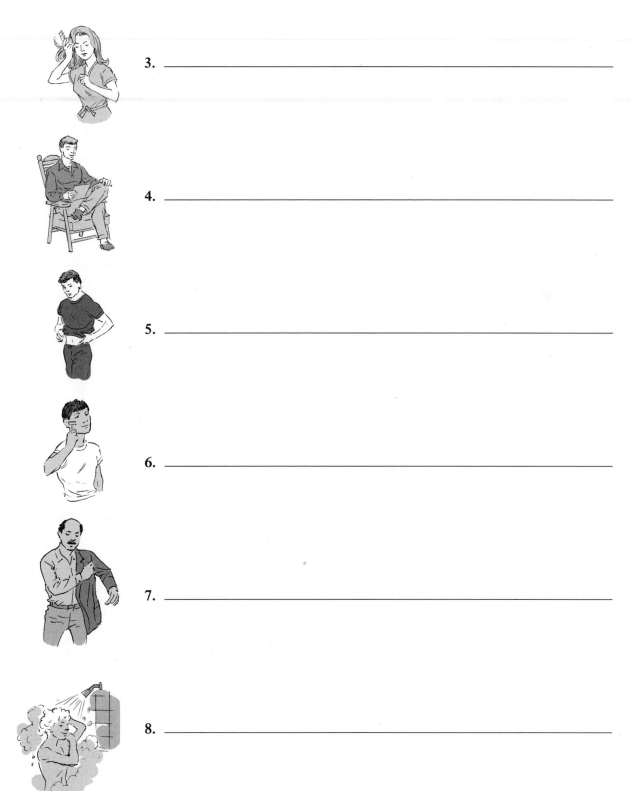

3. _____

4. _____

5. _____

6. _____

7. _____

8. _____

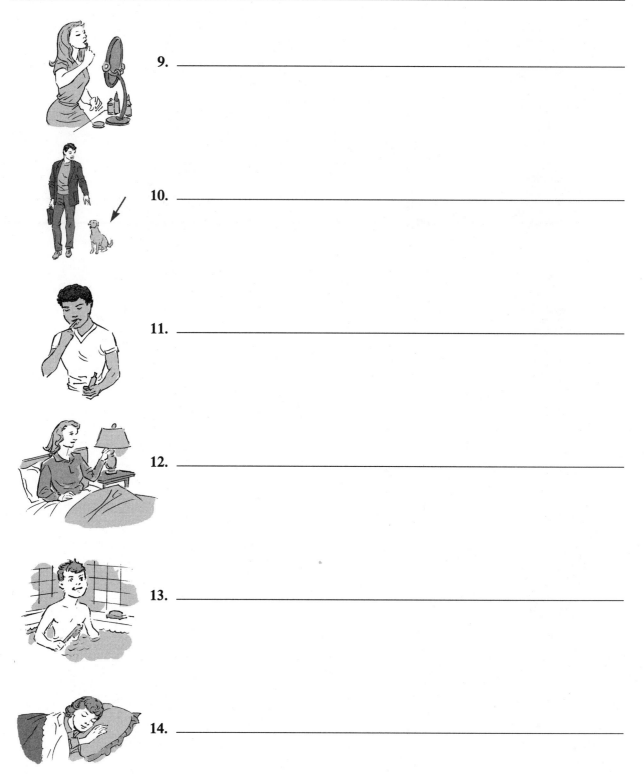

9. _____

10. _____

11. _____

12. _____

13. _____

14. _____

15. _____

16. _____

17. _____

18. _____

19. _____

D. Answer each question about your daily habits using the **yo** form of the reflexive verb.

¿A qué hora te despiertas por la mañana?

Yo me despierto a las siete de la mañana.

1. ¿A qué hora te levantas por la mañana?

2. ¿A qué hora te vas a la escuela por la mañana?

3. ¿A qué hora te acuestas por la noche?

4. ¿Te vistes rápidamente o lentamente por la mañana?

5. ¿Qué ropa te pones para ir a una fiesta?

6. ¿Te diviertes mucho en las fiestas?

7. ¿Siempre te maquillas o te afeitas por la mañana?

8. ¿Siempre te cepillas los dientes por la mañana?

9. ¿Siempre te peinas por la mañana?

10. ¿Prefieres bañarte o ducharte?

11. ¿Siempre te lavas las manos antes de comer?

_____

12. ¿Te despides de tu madre antes de irte a la escuela?

_____

13. ¿Te gusta quedarte en casa los fines de semana o prefieres irte de la casa?

_____

E. Now that we know about you, tell about your best friend. Answer the questions above as they apply to him or her.

1. _____

2. _____

3. _____

4. _____

5. _____

6. _____

7. _____

8. _____

9. _____

10. _____

11. _____

12. _____

13. _____

Nombre _____

ESTRUCTURA *Making descriptive adverbs from adjectives, Comparison of adverbs*

F. Compare how the two people mentioned do things. First choose an adjective from the list below and add the **mente** ending to make an adverb. Then use a comparison to describe how these people do things. Don't forget to change the **o** to **a** before adding **mente**.

especial	inmediato	curioso	posible	público
final	necesario	feliz	cómodo	sincero
inteligente	nervioso	generoso	incorrecto	triste
ambicioso	perfecto	fácil	lento	raro
correcto	rápido	frecuente	perezoso	tímido

Juan vive… María

*Juan vive más cómodamente que María.*

1. El dentista trabaja… el mecánico

   _____

2. El profesor habla español… el estudiante

   _____

3. El atleta corre… un caballo

   _____

4. La cantante canta… un pájaro

   _____

5. Geraldo estudia… Marisela

   _____

6. El perro come… un elefante

   _____

7. La actriz se viste… yo

   _____

8. El periodista escribe… un niño

   _____

9. Y yo… *[make up your own!]*

   _____

LEEMOS Y CONTAMOS

G. The extraterrestrial wrote a letter about his daily routine on his planet. After you have read it, answer the questions about him that follow.

Querido terrestre,

¿Deseas saber cómo es la rutina diaria en mi planeta? Es muy normal y aburrida pero aquí tienes una descripción.

Me levanto a la una de la tarde porque dormimos durante el día. Me cepillo los dedos y me maquillo los pies. Me ducho con ácido líquido, me afeito el estómago y me peino con un lápiz. Luego me pongo un sombrero en la espalda, me despido del refrigerador y me voy al volcán a trabajar. Después del trabajo me lavo el estómago y me siento en el techo para divertirme con cálculos de álgebra. A las diez de la mañana yo me acuesto en el baño, me duermo con los ojos abiertos y me quedo allí por dos horas. Y finalmente me despierto al mediodía.

¿Es tu rutina diaria igual o un poco diferente?

Adiós terrestre.

1. When does the extraterrestrial go to bed, and when does he get up?

_____

2. Describe his morning routine. How does he get dressed?

_____

3. What does he say good-bye to, and where does he go to work?

_____

4. What does he do for fun after work?

_____

5. How does he go to sleep, and how long does he stay there?

_____

H. **¡Ahora te toca a ti!** Pretend you have landed on another planet and want to report on the daily routine there. Do they live like we do or are they a little different like our extraterrestrial was? Use the **ellos se...** forms of the reflexive verbs.

_____

_____

_____

_____

_____

_____

_____

_____

_____

DIVERSIÓN

On a separate sheet of paper, describe in detail your typical school day. Then plan what the ideal day for you will be.

LA REALIDAD	LA FANTASÍA
Me despierto a las cinco de la mañana.	*Me despertaré a las nueve de la mañana.*
Me levanto a las cinco y cinco.	*Me levantaré a las nueve y media.*
Me baño a las cinco y diez.	*Me bañaré a las diez.*

Nombre_____

✦ Unidad IV Lección 6 ✦

Salimos de vacaciones
We're leaving on vacation

VOCABULARIO **De vacaciones** *On vacation*

A. Write at least five things you and a friend can do in each of the following scenes.

1. ___*Podemos decidir en una destinación.*_____

_____

_____

_____

_____

_____

_____

255

2. _____*Podemos descansar.*_____

_____

_____

_____

_____

_____

_____

_____

_____

_____

_____

_____

_____

3. _Podemos conocer a la gente._

4. _Podemos ir a la playa._

VOCABULARIO   La ropa *Clothing*

B. What do you wear in each of these situations? Answer using vocabulary from the lesson.

to go boating

Yo llevo unos pantalones cortos y una camiseta.

1. to go to a party

2. when it rains

3. when getting ready to go to bed

4. when it's hot outside

5. when going to work

6. when going to a wedding

7. in the winter

ESTRUCTURA *Summary of irregular verbs*

C. Choose a verb from the list below whose meaning fits the sentence. Then complete each sentence with the correct <u>preterite</u>, <u>present</u>, and <u>future</u> forms of the verb. (There may be more than one verb whose meaning fits the sentence.)

hacer *(to do/make)*	poder *(to be able/can)*
tener *(to have)*	decir *(to say/tell)*
venir *(to come)*	poner *(to put)*
salir *(to leave)*	querer *(to want/love)*
estar *(to be)*	ir *(to go)*
ser *(to be)*	saber *(to know)*

Preterite: Yo ____*tuve*_____ un perro.

Present: _____*tengo*_____

Future: _____*tendré*_____

1. Preterite: Yo _____ la verdad.

   Present: _____

   Future: _____

2. Preterite: Yo _____ la comida.

   Present: _____

   Future: _____

3. Preterite: Yo _____ tu libro en la mesa.

   Present: _____

   Future: _____

4. Preterite: Yo _____ al hotel a las ocho de la mañana.

   Present: _____

   Future: _____

5. Preterite: Yo nunca _____ tarde para la clase.

   Present: _____

   Future: _____

6. Preterite: Yo _____ de mi casa a las siete de la mañana.

   Present: _____

   Future: _____

7. Preterite: Yo no _____ venir a tu fiesta.

   Present: _____

   Future: _____

8. Preterite: Yo nunca _____ cuántos años tiene el profesor.

   Present: _____

   Future: _____

9. Preterite: Yo _____ que salir inmediatamente.

   Present: _____

   Future: _____

10. Preterite: Yo _____ estudiante en esta escuela.

    Present: _____

    Future: _____

11. Preterite: Yo _____ con Uds. al parque.

    Present: _____

    Future: _____

LEEMOS Y CONTAMOS

D. Paulina and her friends are discussing what they like to do on vacation. Read what they say and then answer the questions that follow.

PAULINA   En mis vacaciones me gusta hacer un viaje largo a un lugar exótico donde puedo broncearme en la playa. También me gusta nadar y recoger conchas. Pero los billetes de avión cuestan mucho.

PEDRO   Para mí es más agradable pasar las vacaciones en una ciudad porque me gusta visitar museos, comer en restaurantes, ir al teatro y a conciertos, ver los monumentos y edificios grandes e ir de compras en las tiendas.

LOLITA   Pues, yo prefiero unas vacaciones más tranquilas. Me gusta ir a nuestra casa de campo para estar al aire libre, mirando los animales, pescando en el río y sacando fotos de las flores.

CHARLIE   ¡Uds. no saben descansar en sus vacaciones! Yo simplemente me quedo en casa en mis vacaciones. Así no tengo que decidir en una destinación, comprar billetes, gastar dinero, hacer las maletas, decir adiós a los amigos, comprar recuerdos ni enviar tarjetas postales. Además, ¡no tengo que contarles a Uds. de mis aventuras cuando vuelvo de las vacaciones!

PAULINA   ¡Y eso es porque tú eres una persona tan aburrida!

1. What does Paulina like to do on her vacation?

_____

_____

_____

_____

2. Where does Pedro like to go? Why?

_____

_____

_____

_____

3. What about Lolita?

_____

_____

_____

_____

4. What does Charlie like to do, and what does he think the advantages are?

_____

_____

_____

_____

5. What does Paulina think about Charlie's vacation ideas?

_____

_____

_____

_____

E. Where do you like to go and what do you prefer to do on your vacation? (Answer in Spanish.)

_____

_____

_____

_____

_____

_____

_____

DIVERSIÓN

Make a list of the ways that you could use Spanish during your summer vacation.

I could talk to my friends in Spanish.

❧ Unidad IV Structure Review ❧

PAULINA, SU FAMILIA Y SUS AMIGOS

Note: Review Tools section in the textbook at the beginning of Unit IV before doing the activities in this Unit summary.

Personal a *(Lesson 1)*

A. **¡Qué desastre!**   Paulina's alarm went off at what she thought was the usual time, but she had a surprise when she got to Rosita's house. Here is what happened. Add the *personal* **a** where necessary.

Durante la noche se fue la electricidad y el reloj no despertó _____ Paulina a tiempo.

1

Paulina no sabía que no tenían _____ electricidad durante la noche y no sabía que

2

había salido *(had left)* tarde para la escuela. Primero, fue en su bicicleta a casa de Rosita.

Esperó _____ Rosita en frente de la casa, pero no vio ni _____ Rosita ni_____

3 4 5

su hermana. No había nadie en la casa. ¡Qué extraño! No vio _____ nadie cerca de la

6

escuela. Miró _____ su reloj pulsera. Paulina se sorprendió *(was surprised)*. Eran las

7

diez de la mañana. Estaba atrasada *(delayed)* más de dos horas.

Nombre_____

Object pronouns (Lessons 1, 2)

B. **¿Qué necesita para la clase?** When Paulina arrived at school, she went to her locker and had to decide what to take with her to math class. Using pronouns, tell whether she took each of the items indicated.

el lápiz mecánico ___*Paulina lo llevó.*___

las botas ___*No las llevó.*___

1. el bolígrafo _____

2. el globo _____

3. la calculadora _____

4. la guitarra _____

5. los pantalones cortos _____

6. los cuadernos _____

7. las cintas de pronunciación _____

8. las fotos de una fiesta _____

C. **¿Qué nota recibirán?** Mrs. Watson, the math teacher, has calculated grades for her students. Using the grading system used in your school, give these people their grades based on their percentage.

Paulina: 99% ___*La señora Watson le dió una A.*___

Tomás y Ramón: 97% ___*La señora Watson les dió una A.*___

1. Rosita 96% _____

2. Inés y Dorotea 92% _____

3. Salvador 89% _____

4. Jaime y Roberto 86% _____

5. el muchacho pelirrojo 81% _____

6. la muchacha détras de él 74% _____

7. Raúl 72% _____

D. No hay mal que por bien no venga. *Every cloud has a silver lining.* The morning's disaster turns to good fortune for Paulina. Fill in the appropriate direct and indirect object pronouns while you find out how the power outage saved the day for Paulina.

Cuando Paulina llegó a la escuela, Rosita estuvo muy contenta de ver _____ .
1

_____ saludó y _____ dió los apuntes que hizo en las clases.
2   3

—¿Qué _____ pasó?— _____ preguntó Rosita. Paulina
4   5

contestó, —No sé, mi reloj no _____ despertó hasta las nueve.— —Ah, sí, —
6

respondió Rosita. —Se fue la electricidad y eso _____ causó problemas a
7

muchas personas. Pues, la señorita Blanco no _____ *(to us)* dió el examen
8

hoy. Dice que _____ dará mañana.— —Ay, Dios mío,— exclamó Paulina.—
9

¡ _____ olvidé! Ahora tengo esta noche para estudiar. ¡ _____
10   11

salvó la falta de electricidad!

Reflexive pronouns (Lesson 5)

E. Una mañana típica en la casa de los Rodríguez Paulina's family has a daily routine. Is it different from yours? Complete with the correct reflexive pronouns.

_____ despertamos muy temprano en mi casa. Mi papá _____ despierta
1   2

a las cinco y veinte y mi mamá _____ despierta diez minutos más tarde. Después
3

de levantar_____ , mi mamá viene a mi alcoba y me dice: —Paulina,
4

apúra _____ *(hurry)*, tienes que despertar _____ ahora.
5   6

No _____ levanto inmediatamente. Mis hermanos casi siempre están en el
7

cuarto de baño cuando _____ levanto. Ellos tienen que afeitar_____ y
8   9

peinar_____ antes de salir del cuarto de baño, y no escuchan cuando yo grito:
10

—Roberto, Pablo, háganme el favor *(please)* de apurar_____ . Yo tengo que
11

duchar_____ , peinar_____ , maquillar_____ y
12   13   14

vestir _____ .
15

No sé cómo puedo preparar_____ para ir a la escuela en solamente quince
16

minutos, pero lo hago y nunca llego tarde. Pues… casi nunca.

Position of object pronouns (Lesson 1)

F. **Una sorpresa para mamá** Paulina's mother went to visit her cousin in another city. The family has decided to surprise her by doing her chores. First tell that Mamá always does that chore, then tell who is going to do it this week—Papá, Roberto, Pablo, Paulina, Carlota, or cousin Eduardo. Rewrite each sentence, replacing the underlined noun with a pronoun.

lavar <u>la ropa</u> *Mamá siempre la lava.*

Carlota va a lavarla esta semana.

1. comprar <u>la comida</u> _____

   _____

2. cocinar <u>la comida</u> _____

   _____

3. servir (i,i) <u>la comida</u> _____

   _____

4. lavar <u>los platos</u> _____

   _____

5. preparar <u>los almuerzos</u> _____

   _____

6. limpiar <u>la casa</u> _____

   _____

7. coser <u>la ropa</u> _____

   _____

8. escribirles <u>a los abuelos</u> _____

   _____

Double object pronouns (Lesson 2)

G. **¿Qué tienes para el almuerzo, Paulina?** All of Paulina's friends bring their lunches to school. At lunchtime, they often trade food with each other. Paulina was telling her mother about today's trade. Beginning with what the person had, tell to whom he or she gave it.

Jaime tenía una banana.   (a Gloria)

Se la dió a Gloria.
_____

1. Teresa tenía una rosquilla.   (a Jaime)

_____

2. Marta tenía unos panecillos.   (a Teresa y Sara)

_____

3. Salvador tenía una barra de chocolate.   (a Marta)

_____

4. Dorotea tenía una ensalada de zanahorias.   (a Salvador)

_____

5. Rosita tenía unos arándanos.   (a Dorotea y a mí)

_____

6. Inés tenía una tortita de chocolate.   (a Rosita)

_____

7. Yolanda tenía un bocadillo de pollo.   (a Inés)

_____

8. Gloria tenía palomitas de maíz.   (a Yolanda y a mí)

_____

9. Raúl tenía una manzana.   (a mí)

_____

10. Yo tenía dulces de chocolate.   (a todos mis amigos)

_____

-Ar *verb pattern (Lesson 1)*

H. **¿Qué haremos durante el fin de semana?**   The girls have no plans for the weekend.
Write the verbs in the <u>future</u> tense while you discover what their plans are.

—¿Qué (hacer) _____*haremos*_____ nosotros este fin de semana?— preguntó Paulina.

—Yo sé— respondió Inés. —Vamos a dar una fiesta elegante. Nosotros (celebrar)

_____ el cumpleaños de Eduardo. Yo (invitar) _____ a todos
       1   2

nuestros amigos. Yo (limpiar) _____ mi casa y Paulina y Rosita me
                               3

(ayudar) _____ a decorarla. Nosotros (comprar) _____
            4   5

refrescos y papitas fritas. María (preparar) _____ unos sándwiches y Yolanda
                                      6

(preparar) _____ una ensalada. Todo el mundo (llevar) _____
            7   8

discos y Juana (tocar) _____ su guitarra. —¡Qué buena idea!— exclamaron
                       9

todas las muchachas.

I. **Nos divertimos en la fiesta.**   It's Saturday night and everyone is at the party. Use the
<u>preterite</u> tense to tell what they did before and at the party.

Cuando Inés (invitar) _____*invitó*_____ a sus amigos a la fiesta, todos (aceptar)

_____ la invitación. Paulina y Rosita (decorar) _____ la sala
            1   2

con globos y flores. María y Yolanda (preparar) _____ la comida. Los otros
                                      3

amigos (llegar) _____ a las ocho. A las once, todo el mundo le (dar)
                  4

_____ los regalos a Eduardo y le (cantar) _____ «Feliz
            5   6

cumpleaños».

J. En la fiesta Now use the <u>present</u> tense to describe the party.

Todo el mundo (estar) _____ *está* _____ bien vestido. Las muchachas (llevar)

_____₁ pantalones o faldas y los muchachos (llevar) _____₂

camisas deportivas y aún corbatas. ¡Qué fiesta más formal! Todos (escuchar)

_____₃ la música. —Yo (desear) _____₄ bailar contigo— le dice

Juan a Yolanda.—Y yo (aceptar)_____₅ tu invitación— le (contestar)

_____₆ Yolanda; y Juan y Yolanda (bailar) _____₇ .—Nosotros

(bailar) _____₈ bien juntos— dice Juan. —Sí,— responde Yolanda.

K. La fiesta de anoche Sunday morning Paulina tells her brothers Roberto and Tomás about last night's party. (Use the <u>preterite</u>.)

Anoche mis amigos y yo (celebrar) _____₁ el cumpleaños de Eduardo.

Todo el mundo (aceptar) _____₂ nuestra invitación y fue bien vestido. Yo

(llegar) _____₃ a las siete y (ayudar) _____₄ con las

decoraciones. María (preparar) _____₅ los bocadillos y Yolanda (preparar)

_____₆ una ensalada grande. Todas nosotras (comprar)

_____₇ los refrescos, chips y una torta de cumpleaños. Todo el mundo

(escuchar) _____₈ la música y (bailar) _____₉ . Claro,

yo (bailar) _____₁₀ mucho con Salvador. Nosotros (saludar)

_____₁₁ a nuestros amigos y (tomar) _____₁₂ refrescos.

Más tarde, le (presentar) _____₁₃ los regalos a Eduardo y le (cantar)

_____₁₄ «Feliz cumpleaños».

L. Abuelita iba a las fiestas también. The Rodríguez children like to hear stories about the past from their grandparents. Abuelita told them about the **quinceañeros** she used to go to when she was a teenager. (Use the <u>imperfect</u>.)

Cuando yo (ser) _____ joven, (ir) _____ a muchas fiestas de
          1   2

quinceañera. Cuando las muchachas (llegar) _____ a la edad de quince años,
                                               3

(celebrar) _____ este cumpleaños con una fiesta especial. Primero, había una
            4

misa en la iglesia, donde (dar) _____ las gracias. Sus padres, toda su familia y
                                  5

sus amigos la (acompañar) _____ a la iglesia. Ellas (llevar) _____
                            6   7

un vestido muy elegante. Después de la misa, todo el mundo (celebrar) _____
                                                                        8

con una cena en la casa de la muchacha o en un restaurante. De vez en cuando había músicos

que (tocar) _____ y todo el mundo (bailar) _____ . Yo siempre
             9   10

(ir) _____ a las fiestas con mis padres porque en esos días las muchachas no
      11

(participar) _____ en actividades sociales sin una chaperona.
              12

-Er and -ir verb pattern (Lesson 3)

M. ¿Cuándo, cuándo, cuándo? Complete the sentences with the correct forms of the verbs. Be careful to use the appropriate tense.

Para el postre, Mamá (comer) _comía_ tortas de chocolate pero ahora _come_

fruta. Anoche _comió_ una pera y esta noche _comerá_ una manzana.

1. De niño, Juan (vivir) _____ en México pero ahora

_____ en Chicago. A causa del trabajo de su padre, el año

pasado _____ en Detroit, y el próximo año

_____ en Pittsburgh.

2. Hace tres años, nosotros (asistir) _____ a la escuela primaria,

pero ahora _____ a la escuela secundaria. Antes siempre

_____ a todas las clases. En cinco años

_____ a la universidad.

3. En la escuela primaria, yo (leer) _____ cuentos fáciles, pero

ahora que estoy en la secundaria, _____ cuentos difíciles.

Ayer _____ un cuento español, y en tres años

_____ libros enteros en español.

4. Cuando tenías tres años, ¿(beber) _____ mucha leche? ¿Qué

_____ tú ahora? ¿ _____ refrescos

anoche? ¿Qué _____ con la merienda?

5. En el pasado, mis hermanos gemelos (recibir) _____ juguetes

de regalo para su cumpleaños. Ahora _____ ropa y libros.

Ayer fue su cumpleaños y _____ camisas y corbatas idénticas.

A los cincuenta años, ¿qué crees tú que _____ ?

Double-verb construction (Lesson 2)

N. **¿Tienes planes para el fin de semana?** Everyone Paulina knows is busy this weekend. Complete these sentences to tell what everyone else is doing.

Roberto debe... *lavar el coche.* _____

1. Pablo espera... _____

2. Raúl necesita... _____

3. Rosita aprende a... _____

4. Salvador acaba de... _____

5. Inés vuelve a... _____

6. Fernando tiene que... _____

7. Carlota puede... _____

8. Eduardo sabe... _____

Compañeros, Spanish for Communication, Book 1
Cuaderno de actividades

UNIDAD IV   Structure Review   273

Stem-changing verbs (Lesson 4)

O. La época de los exámenes Paulina and her friends are busy with final exams. These exams are very important for their grades in their classes, and everyone is very concerned about doing well. Complete the sentences with the correct forms of the present tense of the verbs. Some of the verbs are <u>stem-changing</u>, others are not. Be careful!

Por ser buenos estudiantes que (desear) _____ asistir a una universidad, todo
                                          1

el mundo (querer) _____ recibir una buena nota en los exámenes. Por eso,
                          2

durante la época de exámenes, mis amigos no (practicar) _____ deportes.
                                                                3

Nosotros no (dormir) _____ bien durante la noche antes de un examen porque
                            4

(estudiar) _____ mucho. Algunas veces, algunos amigos (estudiar)
                  5

_____ conmigo y mi mamá nos (servir) _____ café con galletas.
        6   7

El día del examen, yo (llevar) _____ muchos lápices y generalmente hay
                                      8

otro estudiante que me (pedir) _____ un lápiz porque no (tener)
                                      9

_____ ninguno. Cuando el profesor (entrar) _____ en la clase,
        10   11

nosotros (cerrar) _____ los libros y el examen (comenzar)
                        12

_____ . El profesor nos (dar) _____ las instrucciones y nos
        13   14

las (repetir) _____ para estar seguro que todo el mundo las (comprender)
                    15

_____ .
        16

El aula (estar) _____ muy callada mientras todos los estudiantes (pensar)
                        17

_____ en las respuestas. Nosotros no (pensar) _____ en otras
        18   19

cosas durante el examen. Es muy importante (recordar) _____ las respuestas.
                                                              20

Porque (estudiar) _____ mucho, nosotros (poder) _____ salir
                          21   22

bien en los exámenes.

Después del examen, mis amigos y yo (almorzar) _____ juntos para discutir
                                                        23

el examen y entonces (volver) _____ a la clase. Todo el mundo
                                      24

(considerar) _____ que los exámenes son muy importantes.
                    25

P. Los exámenes del año pasado Complete the paragraph with the correct forms of the verbs in the <u>preterite</u> tense.

Los estudiantes le (pedir) _____ al profesor un examen fácil, pero él siempre
1

les (dar) _____ un examen difícil. Ellos no se (divertir) _____
2   3

en esos exámenes porque (preferir) _____ un examen más fácil. Yo nunca
                                                    4

(dormir) _____ bien. Bueno... nadie (dormir) _____ bien antes
                  5   6

de uno de sus exámenes.

Irregular verbs

Q. Paulina and her friends are studying for their final exam in Spanish. They have decided to review the irregular verbs. Help them by writing the following verbs in these tenses.

		YO PRESENT	NOSOTROS FUTURE	ELLOS PRETERITE	ÉL IMPERFECT
	ser	*soy*	*seremos*	*fueron*	*era*
1.	tener				
2.	ir				
3.	venir				
4.	traer				
5.	hacer				
6.	dar				
7.	salir				
8.	poner				
9.	decir				
10.	oír				
11.	ver				
12.	conocer				
13.	saber				
14.	querer				
15.	poder				

Adverbs (Lesson 5)

R. **¿Cómo trabajan?** Everyone has his or her own way of working. Here are the work styles of Paulina's friends. Write the correct adverb to describe them.

(rápido) Paulina trabaja ___*rápidamente.*___

1. (perfecto) Rosita trabaja _____.

2. (cuidadoso) Salvador trabaja _____.

3. (independiente) Los hermanos Calderón trabajan _____.

4. (diligente) Todos los amigos trabajan _____.

Comparison of adverbs (Lesson 5)

S. **¿Cómo trabajan otros?** Inés, Dorotea, and Raúl are doing their math together. Compare the manner in which the friends work.

Inés termina primero, Raúl termina segundo y Dorotea termina tercero.

___*Inés trabaja más rápidamente que Raúl y Dorotea trabaja menos*___

___*rápidamente que Raúl.*___

1. Raúl tiene más problemas correctos e Inés tiene menos problemas correctos.

   Raúl trabaja _____

   _____.

2. Dorotea es muy seria, Inés es menos seria y Raúl no es serio.

   Dorotea trabaja _____

   _____.

3. Inés es inteligente. Raúl es más inteligente. Dorotea es la más inteligente de la clase.

   Inés trabaja _____

   _____.

Use of adjective with article without the noun (Lesson 4)

T. **Vamos a salir de vacaciones.**   Now that exams are over, it's time to think about vacation. What are some things that one has to consider when going on vacation? Complete the following sentences.

1. Lo importante es _____.

2. Lo práctico es _____.

3. Lo difícil es _____.

4. Lo fácil es _____.

5. Lo triste es _____.

U. Paulina has choices to make about her vacation. Help her decide what to do.

Paulina puede tomar una vacación cara o una vacación barata.

_Paulina tomará la barata._____

1. Paulina puede llevar la maleta grande o la maleta pequeña.

   Paulina llevará _____.

2. Paulina puede llevar la ropa deportiva o la ropa formal.

   Paulina llevará _____.

3. Ella puede llevar la falda azul o la falda amarilla.

   Ella llevará _____.

4. Ella puede visitar a las amigas mexicanas o a las amigas cubanas.

   Ella visitará a _____.

5. Puede comprarles un regalo barato o un regalo caro.

   Comprará _____.

Negative expressions (Lesson 4)

V. Rosita couldn't remember what Pablo and María had told her about their vacations. She asks Paulina for verification and finds out she was completely wrong. Answer her questions using the negatives for the underlined words.

¿Alguien va a viajar con Pablo?

No, nadie va a viajar con Pablo.

1. ¿Pablo va siempre al Perú durante las vacaciones?

_____

2. ¿Pablo va a visitar a alguien en el Perú?

_____

3. ¿María va al Perú también?

_____

4. ¿Tienen algunos amigos en el Perú?

_____

5. ¿Desea Pablo ir en junio o en julio?

_____

6. ¿Le comprará Pablo algo para su tía?

_____